# Believe in Spirit

## You are spirit in human form

*Written by Steve Bridger*
*Channelled by Janet Neville*

Clink
Street

Published by Clink Street Publishing 2021

Copyright © 2021

First edition.

ISBN:
978-1-913962-41-8 - paperback
978-1-913962-42-5 - ebook

**We would like to dedicate this book to Our Spirit Guides and:**

Janet's children:

Lucy & Paul
And to the rest of the family for their love and support

Steve's children:

Brean & Jack

Steve's Mum:

Edna Lucy Bridger

**In Loving Memory of:**

Patsy Wood, Debbie Neville and Mary Gooding

**Heartfelt thanks to:**

Louise Wood

Cindy Theodore

Rosie Halliday

Suzi Cartwright

Tracy Maher

Allan Watt

Wendy Harvey

spirit@beingspirits.com
https://www.beingspirits.com

# Contents

# Contents

# Reader Reactions

## An Inspiration

"Well, I've made good use of the afternoon. Katie went to the shops, my youngest daughter went to her room, and I finished off your book!

I have to say, it's far more satisfying to devour it in large chunks. It also gives you a better sense of the structure, which I thought was spot on. By devoting large parts of the book to certain 'large' subjects - like reincarnation, and what happens when we pass over - the reader really gets the chance the immerse themself in the material.

Speaking for myself, I got the most from the descriptions of passing over, and beyond. Some aspects - such as the life review - I was familiar with already, but most of it I wasn't. It's riveting stuff, made all the more convincing - and reassuring - by the verbatim reports from Spirit.

Talking of which ... it was an inspired decision to include messages from Spirit. Not only do they inform and reinforce the purpose and point of the book, they break it up and give the layout some variety, which aids readability.

And that's about it, really. It's a thought-provoking and stimulating book, allowing us not only to imagine our future beyond this incarnation, but giving us the opportunity to influence that future by reviewing - and perhaps changing - how we currently live our life.

It was an honour to read it, Steve. Pass on my thanks to Janet. I wish you both the greatest success!"

Much peace and love,
Gordon Robertson

Steve Bridger & Janet Neville

# Welcome Friend

## Introduction

This book is about your personal, innermost, spirituality.

*'Believe in Spirit'* is about love and learning, of peace of mind, of inner contentment. It is about realising who you are and believing in the uniqueness of you.

You are spirit in human form. You are a spiritual being.

The achievement of the human spirit is on display every single day. An incredible example of this is the super-human achievement of Sarah Thomas from the USA. Sarah is a cancer survivor. On the 17th September 2019, Sarah swam the English Channel *four times non-stop,* covering a distance of some 130 miles over a 54 hour period. It was a supreme act of will. People demonstrate courage, resilience and fortitude to overcome insurmountable odds. They draw upon their inner strength of spirit.

This book has been written in an uncomplicated way as two friends talking together. You will learn about the world of spirit and your place within it. You are an everlasting life-force. The lessons have been received direct and unchanged from a team of spirit guides. The authors have acted as go-betweens. This is not a work of fiction. It speaks to mankind's core spirituality. Spirituality that's common to every human being regardless of colour, creed or religion. Spirituality is the essence of our being and the emotional bond between us, this beautiful planet, and the world of spirit.

## We Live in Two Parallel Worlds - The Material and the Spiritual

We live in parallel worlds, two interconnected realities. Our reality, our earth, is the physical domain of the human spirit. The world of spirit is an invisible state of pure energy, driven by thought, of love and peace. It is a separate reality entwined with our own. The two worlds exist side by side at one and the same time. We are currently living on the earth plane. When our time on earth is over our spirit ascends from our physical bodies and continues as consciousness; as indestructible mental energy.

The knowledge in *Believe in Spirit* has been transferred from a number of spiritual minds to the mind of Janet Neville. Janet is a Spiritual Medium. She acts as a channel of communication between our two worlds. The messages are written down exactly as received from spirit, for us to learn about our spirituality and the workings of spirit within our daily lives.

Our teachers are a group of eight Native American Indian guides. They instigated the *'Being Spirit'* programme of learning with the first book in the series. The group of eight are joined by other highly evolved spirits who contribute on various subjects. Sharing of knowledge is at the heart of everything they do. Spirit wants to enlighten us and for us to enlighten others, and hopefully, for you to share this knowledge when you feel the time is right. You will be meeting many spirit guides throughout the book. We give their names and our thanks for being with us.

## Cast away fear and doubt

It takes strength and courage to cast away fear of the unknown. To think this wide about spirit, to open your inner self to ideas that go against everything you've been taught since you can remember takes bravery. To go against the norm leaves you open to ridicule. There comes a time when you question received wisdom. When you look to the skies and sense a yearning to step across the line to explore the unthinkable. Your mind has brought you to this point. This is an opportunity to go deeper and ask questions of your very existence.

It is fear of the unknown that can stop you in your tracks. Don't be scared. Leave the fear behind.

## Being Spirit – Book One

This is how the first *Being Spirit* book came as described by spirit. These are their words:

"The whole purpose of this venture is one that has been in discussion for a long time. There are many written words about our world. People choose to write on various subjects which are close to their hearts. There have been many written words on angels. There are numerous writings on how angels help and protect and can transcend from spirit to earth in the wake of atrocities to help lessen the trauma from the terrors which occur on your earth.

There are many written words about the realms of spirit; how in each realm there are spheres and planes, how a spirit has to work towards reaching each level, how a spirit does not stop learning. A spirit is always learning and evolving towards the Divine Light. It is all there on many written pages.

This was all in a discussion until the spirit named Blue Flame spoke out and mentioned that, although every possible avenue had been placed on parchment, there was something missing, which were pages filled with the written words in simplistic terms. Where a person who is interested in our world would be able to gain a glimpse into how our world is shaped."

Janet acts as messenger to pass on their thoughts and advice. She creates a clear pathway to allow their wisdom to flow.

## A Two Part Book

The first part of this book concerns our material lifetime as spirits in human form. The second part will introduce you to the world of spirit. Spirit will shine a light on what follows after your time on earth reaches its natural close.

Spirit is within each and every one of us, it is the God particle; the eternal element of our existence. Our material lives are time limited. Our spiritual lives are endless. Our souls develop with every earthly experience from the first incarnation to this one. With each rebirth you will experience different lifetimes and different emotional and spiritual challenges. This is to know that we are all evolving spiritually over volumes of time to become as one with the Divine Light.

## Life & the Afterlife: Two halves of the whole

The first earth-life chapters concern your identity as a human spirit with the accent on living fulfilling, positive, joyful lives. The second part is dedicated to their world. You will learn about the realms of spirit and what it's like to live in a world of infinite energy where your thoughts shape your reality.

As John Lennon said:

"I'm not afraid of death because I don't believe in it. It's just getting out of one car, and into another."

As a human spirit you are already a player, already a participant, in a spiritual state for longer than you know. You are an indestructible being of thought energy. Spirit is the life force inside you. Consciousness exists beyond the material world. When your physical body dies your spirit and your soul lives on. Spirit guides are our invisible friends. We are them. They are us. They have lived as we have lived on earth, experiencing emotional highs and lows, heartache and joy during their lifetimes. Just like us.

## Our invisible friends:

"My friend, in our world we want everyone to know the truth that not only is life eternal, but that we are there to help, protect and guide. We can help relieve the pressure from your hectic lives. We can help relieve stress and disharmony. We want people to give a thought to what is beyond your living life, and have a small amount of belief and trust that we will be there in times of stress and hardships. We are your friends. We come with the kind of friendship that blends into the love that only spirit can give. Love is given in its purest form."


## Proof of Spiritual life after physical death

If you'd like immediate proof that consciousness does exist after physical death, you could visit a Spiritualist Church to gain personal evidence. You could witness for yourself the work of a Spiritual Medium, as they use their gift of clairvoyance to link with departed family and friends, either during a public church service or a private reading. Loved ones would introduce themselves and give personal details to confirm their identity and relationship with you. In most cases, a timely and relevant message that is deeply personal will be given. These messages will remind friends and relations of precious times spent together and confirm that they are still present in your life. This is not fortune telling. The single purpose is to prove that life continues after physical death.

These words from the first *Being Spirit* book underscore the communication link between our two worlds:

"Communication from our world to yours is to prove that life is eternal. Human spirit is energy, it is mind and thought. Spirit is indestructible. Spirit lives on continuously. When you are on the earth in a physical body it is easy to forget that you are spirit in human form. You are an everlasting spiritual being. The purpose for us is to produce these written words in the hope that whoever reads this can gain a small amount of understanding about the realms of spirit."

## Spirit's Brief for 'Believe in Spirit'

This message is from Morning Mist. It includes some comments on how spirit would like this second book to be written:

"The whole purpose of Book One was to gain the interest and understanding within the minds of people who have an interest in the afterlife. It is a subject that intrigues and fascinates many but can also place a certain amount of fear and doubt within their minds. Book One has been written with simplicity and clarity and great approval from our world. It will become very successful. People are finding within the pages much wisdom from us and clear and easy reading from your part. It has and will give comfort to many people.

Not at any point are we trying to convert people over onto our way of thinking. It has to be the choice of the individual if they wish to further their education of what is to come when it is their time to return to the homeland. It has become a gentle and thoughtful read for those who have read it, and also for those whom have yet to discover it.

Book Two. We would like our world to be explained in slightly more detail. It is to be a continuation from Book One where you will gradually lead the reader from the earth through the veil to the spiritual realms.

Our thoughts are of you writing as if you are talking to the reader, leading them gently by the hand and taking them on a journey to the world of spirit. It would be like an excursion into places where you can only visit when you have shed your physical body. We want the reader's mind to actually feel as if they are there witnessing first hand of what to expect when the mind realises it is still very much alive but without a physical body and how the spirit has to adjust to the changes it has found itself in.

It's at this point we would like to assure you that we will be there each and every step of the way and will relieve you of any stress that may come upon you. We will simply fade our energies back so you can rest until it is time for you to commence with the writings again. We want people to understand that there is no darkness when a person's life ends, there is light and love and pure happiness.

It's understandable that the physical life form is afraid of the unknown. There are many observations made on your earth as to what happens to the spirit when it has been released from the body. This is what we wish to be explained in simple words. There have been many pages written on this subject. It is with simplicity and clarity we wish our world to be explained for the curious and interested few. It fills us with joy every time we see a light brighten when someone has accepted the fact that we are there watching, waiting and guiding."

My friend our energies are once again pulsating with excitement for the journey ahead. Morning Mist

## Spirit is the love that binds us

The first *Being Spirit* book has been read by followers of many religions and followers of none. The vast majority of people need something to believe in. Spirituality is the one factor that binds us all. The love and strength of the human spirit is fundamental in the positive codes of living we share. This book is for everyone. The love and learning from Spirit touches our hearts and minds. We are all spiritual beings. Your relationship with Spirit is an intensely personal one. The connection of your soul with Spirit is an unbreakable bond.

We hope that this book will help you become more aware of the role of Spirit in your daily life whatever your religion or belief system. We trust that the evidence within these pages will help you find a factor that was possibly missing from your life.

We'll leave the last words of this chapter to Five Arrows, one of the group of eight:

"Our world is in the ether, it's all around the earth's atmosphere and we communicate by the way of thought process. We channel our energies and thoughts onto the energies of working Mediums, in order for us to share our knowledge and spread the word of love and peace throughout your world"

## Coming Next:

We'll begin the earth life chapters. The first concerns the spiritual you. You already bring with you a range of spiritual talents. Everyone has them but not everyone acknowledges or appreciates them. They are the silent drivers of your spirituality and are waiting to be discovered.

# The Earth Life Chapters

PART ONE

The Earth Lore
Chapters

# CHAPTER ONE

# The Spiritual You

You've probably heard this before:

"You only live once. This life is your only life. When you're dead, you're dead."

What if that's wrong?
What if life continues in a state of pure mental energy?
What if spiritual life is everlasting, powered by mind and thought?
What if your spirit is immortal?

This life is one stop, one station, on your spiritual way.

If you knew there's no yawning black hole at the end of the line, how would you live this life? What confidence would it give you? How would you value each and every opportunity? How would you treasure each moment knowing that your 'life sentence' had been lifted? Would you love yourself, your family and friends all the more? Would you forgive those who have hurt you? Would you ask forgiveness from those whom you've hurt? What value would you place on this beautiful planet? Would you want to do more to keep it safe?

Your time on earth is a material and emotional assault course. We all have tests and challenges to overcome. Life is a combination of strife and reward; of bliss and pain, of laughter, joy and tears, of fulfilment and disappointment; and every smile and teardrop in-between.

What may surprise you is that your zigging and zagging pathway of emotions has a plan. This life is when your spirit experiences emotion from before you were born to the moment of passing. Your aspiration is to learn the lessons of this lifetime. You may ask why am I here, what is the meaning of life?

The answer is to live life, to learn, to move closer to spiritual fulfilment, to learn who you really are.


## Your Soul

Your soul captures and records every second of your life. Wang Chang, a highly evolved teaching guide explains:

"The soul is the reflection of human experience while on earth. Your soul is your emotions. Your spirit is your personality. Put the two together and they become one. Your personality is what drives you, your character, the introvert you or the extrovert you. Your emotions are the deep inner you. It's the real you where you feel hurt, love, anger, hate. Combining the two isn't always easy. Sometimes it's difficult for people to express their feelings; sometimes people are all too open, sometimes emotions can be sealed like a locked-up box."

That brings us to the next note from Spirit. It explains the difference between your spirit and your soul. You already know your spirit is eternal, but what of your soul? Running Water added this note about your life on earth:

"You are on the earth for but a short time and in spirit for an eternity. The earthly life is most probably the most important one, for my friend isn't it on your earth where all the mistakes, successes, failures, heartaches and sadness are made? Friendships are made and friendships are broken. There are many lessons to be learned if they can be rectified while still on the earth within a person's mind then the spirit in our world know that the work we are doing to help and guide is not being done in vain."

## Your spiritual gifts

On the day you were born you brought with you a combination of mental and spiritual gifts. The mental elements are fundamental to the way we are; the way our consciousness fulfils all our senses and opens our eyes to the world, the silent signals of good and bad, right and wrong from your conscience, the lightning strike of creative imagination, the priceless emotional bank of memories are all evidence of the powerful life force within you.

Your spiritual gifts may be hidden until you slowly become aware of them. As they develop they will change how you think and act. When they become active they have the potential of totally reframing your life on earth. Everyone possesses these mental and spiritual gifts. Some are detectable when felt or demonstrated, for example when someone displays highly attuned perception or sensitivity skills. Mediums link with spirit using the power of thought energy from the mind.

The mind is the centre of boundless energy flowing to and from Spirit. It is energy that feeds us with knowledge and opens our thoughts to what we can each achieve. When we witness the most beautiful, breath-taking sunset our spirits soar. Our senses are lost in the sublime transcendental pleasure of simply being. Thought energy from the mind is our eternal invisible power.

The memories created during our lifetime are saved within our spiritual knowledge bank to be drawn upon at will.

## The Four Gifts of Intuition

Intuition is immensely powerful. We draw upon it when we instinctively sense something. Our minds send alert signals to our consciousness. This is where the Four Gifts of Intuition come in. They are part of our range of spiritual skills. A Spiritual Medium would have developed these gifts to be able to connect with spirit when they act as a communication channel between our two worlds. A description of Spiritual Mediums and Mediumship will follow shortly, but for now, we'll concentrate on the elements that form the spiritual you.

The Four Gifts of Intuition have the prefix 'Clair' which is the French word for 'clear' these are:

### Clairvoyance:

'Clear-seeing' is when images are visualised in the mind. For a Spiritual Medium, clear-seeing is the ability, with expert training, to visualise and describe the departed spirits who wish to make contact with their loved ones. A description would normally relate to the way the spirit looked in terms of height, weight, visual appearance, hair colour, clothing but also pick up on points of their character, moods and personality. Sometimes the way they spoke, things they said and how they said it would confirm someone's identity.

Additionally, evidence may involve the way a person passed into spirit, for example in a car or motorcycle accident, or through cancer or other medical condition. The Medium could see or get a sense of the trauma involved. Not to cause distress but to provide evidence that spiritual life continues. The searing pain of losing them will be eased knowing that they are safe. After a spirit passes, they are surrounded by love and peace; without stress, without pain. Getting that confirmation will let you know for certain that they will forever be alive to help and guide you. They will always be one thought away.

It is important that clairvoyant readings provide evidential support of the information given by a Medium. This can be at the time of the message or corroborated later when something comes to light to prove the accuracy of what has been given. This is referred to as evidential clairvoyance.

### Clairsentient:

'Clear-feeling' is linked to the sense of touch or feeling. It's when you're sensitive to intuitive sensations from the mind. This may be linked to feelings that are linked with the manner of their passing. A Spiritual Medium may feel a similar pain in their chest to suggest someone died of a heart attack, or they may begin to cough or feel a rasping in the chest if the departed spirit suffered from a respiratory problem. The scent of perfume, tobacco smoke or alcohol or other distinctive smells could be sensed by a Medium during a reading. All these could paint a vivid picture in the mind; the smell of the ocean, the tang of salt spray; any of these could trigger a memory that is significant.

### Clairaudience:

'Clear-hearing' stems from within the mind of the Medium. Voices, words, sounds, or musical tunes or instruments are heard in the head. You may have heard people can hear someone talking to them in their heads. Again, this may be part of a spiritual reading when a Medium asks the departed spirit for more information or clarification. The Medium would tune-in to hear the voice of the person in spirit.

### Claircognisance:

'Clear- knowing' is having a premonition or insight into something that is about to happen without any logical explanation. There are many examples of people recalling such premonitions on the internet if you wanted to search for these happenings.

## Living your best life

Spirituality is about self-belief. Believing in your spiritual self is central to how your pathway will unfold. Take pride in your talents. Take strength from what you have already achieved. Take heart from the prospects ahead. Living a spiritual life means to be at one with the world around you. It is our purpose to protect this planet, the environment, the animal kingdom, the birds of the air and the fish in the seas. Every element of our existence should be a harmonious co-existence. Look up to the wonders of space and know that spirit surrounds us and that we are all inter-dependent.

While you are part of a family and friendship group and while you may follow the teachings of a conventional religion, remember that ultimately you are your own person. This message contains the wisdom and guidance of another spirit:

## Loving the spiritual you

Your spirit is your everlasting state of being. It is the eternal you. It is the circle of energy that will evolve and progress over eons of time. You are your own person, a single, eternal spirit slowly evolving and gaining enlightenment until you are as one with the divine.

As a human spirit you have family and friends. You have a family tree that tracks back in time and maybe siblings, babies and children in the future. Your private timeline rolls on. These present moments are part of your spiritual story and yours alone. Love your solitary self and be aware and celebrate your individual spiritual identity. Your inner self is a source of strength and courage. It is your precious gift and yours alone.

These are the words of Lone Wolf:

"Developing in your world is most probably one of the hardest tasks any spirit has to undertake. The spirit is in the physical form. The physical form then becomes a person, a person with needs, with wants, with decisions and choices to make. Mistakes are made but they are to be learned by. Sometimes they are ignored and are thrown to someone else to take the blame because the giver refuses to take responsibility for their own misdemeanors. Many people act in this manner because of the fear of being rejected, put aside, forgotten; to be alone, to live a life of solitude, never to be part of a group again.

My friend, to live a life of solitude has been greatly misunderstood. It means to be free, in charge of one's own spirit; to be able to mix and converse with people in a way where you have no worries or misconceptions about themselves. For them to be prepared for the paths ahead, to be able to open and shut doors when the need arises, to like and to be completely comfortable within themselves and never to be afraid of being alone. You never are alone when you have chosen this pathway because the only person who you have come to rely upon is yourself and no one else. It takes strength and courage to get to this level of living. It brings rewards it means you have discovered your own identity, your true self."

During a recent session with spirit we asked Running Water how they saw us. This was his reply:

"Look up into the blue-blackness of the night sky. You'll see the glittering light of stars and planets. Some are distant tiny pricks of light with scarcely a glow and barely visible. Others are in groups or single points of brightness of different sizes.

That is how we see you. It is your spirit light that shines bright. We see your light not your physical body."

## Shine your light

Your spirituality shines like a homing beacon. It's your Divine Light that Spirit sees. Spirit doesn't see your physical, material form. They are responsive to the auric energy you emit. Happiness and positivity shine brightly. This is especially so when you direct your mental energy toward them and their world. We are spirits upon an earthly stage. By thinking of them we bridge that gap. Our spirit is calling home.

We've asked our guides to describe what they see when viewing us. The answer is in the sky above, in the vista of stars, planets and glorious celestial activity. See the millions of tiny dots of light above the wisps of clouds. To Spirit we are tiny dots sending out spiritual signals of light. Their brightness is an indication of how we are feeling, elated or depressed; the beam can flow from cloudy and dull to sparklingly bright.

In our minds, we know that light conquers dark. That being downcast darkens our mood. That turning on the light of hope we can crawl away from despair. Smiling, helping, hugging directs light to those in need; they inject light into dark. Your light is your human spirit working in unison with the universe. Your kindness and consideration is a powerful restorative tonic to every element of the world around us.

The next time you're feeling low and night is drawing close around you, look out into the sky. Instead of tracts of darkness see the million upon million points of shining light and take comfort. Spirit is with you always.

## Your higher self is the spiritual you

Nobody's perfect. We're all work-in-progress. It's the work you do that will eventually result in reaching and becoming your higher self. You'll look your spiritual self in the mirror and be stunned at the starlight staring back at you. By then you will be the complete article.

You've already had evidence of sublime fulfilment. The heart-pumping emotions of the pure joy of love in all its forms, of personal achievement, of witnessing others reacting to the help you've given, of losing yourself in the beauty of this natural world. Draw on those memories to defeat days of depression, doubt and insecurity. They don't deserve to be remembered. Shake them off like sand in your shoe. The future is there, waiting for you to arrive with a wave of positive electric energy.

Here are some ideas to revitalise your higher self:

1. Forgiveness exercises are good for the soul. They make you feel so much lighter, you can sense the baggage dropping away. Forgive those who have upset or hurt you. Ask for forgiveness from those whom you've damaged. If you can't do it face-to-face, or via some techno device, walk outside into nature and shout 'I'm sorry'. This could be an option if the person you want to forgive or gain forgiveness from is deceased.

2. Have a good talk with yourself. Be honest. Drop those habits or annoying things you do that drive your friends mad. At the same time, tell yourself off for not having the confidence to stand up for yourself. It's about time people saw your light shining again.

3. Complete at least one random act of kindness a day. Ideally, something that will come as a complete surprise to the recipient. Take no payment, apart from a 'Thank You'. Keep this event secret. It is so sweet when only you know what you've done. It's a delightfully private sensation.

4. Prioritise one day at a time. Live life in the 'now' and don't waste this special moment in planning for a next that may never come in the way you expect. Remember the saying 'Today is the tomorrow you worried about yesterday'. By that we mean that nothing moves forward except the passage of time.

5. Fill your soul with positive thoughts. Put your senses on alert to appreciate the beauty around you. Slow down and make more time for yourself. Listen to music, see a show, take a walk in the woods, wonder at the stars above your head, hug someone, fall in love. Feel alive!

Human spirit is an invisible life-force. It transcends the mortal into the immortal as state of mind energy. The core belief of spirituality is that our spirit continues to exist and communicate by the power of thought. Our intelligence and consciousness are evident during our material lives on earth; the human psyche continues to function in the world of spirit. Your spirit lives on. Evidence is received from the spirit world, in the words of Running Water:

"There is only one form of language or communication in spirit and that is thought. The language of Spirit is universal in our world. We do not speak in different tongues because we have left that physical form behind. When a medium is connecting with a loved one in spirit, who would have spoken in a different tongue to the Medium, then the spirit guide will translate the words into the language which the Medium would understand."

**Coming Next:**

The spiritual 'you' is never alone. You have a celestial support network of Guides and Angels forever on call. They are your teachers, supporters, councillors and friends. Think of your guides as close spiritual friends. You have one guide who is particularly close to you and who is always with you. More guides will join you as time goes by.

**CHAPTER TWO**

# Spirit Guides

Spirit Guides were once breathing this air, walking on this soil and living this life. They experienced a mortal existence. When they passed into spirit, they took the decision to continue developing their skills, eventually reaching a point where they were given the responsibility to help guide a soul on earth. That soul could be you. Time as we know it does not exist in the spirit world. There are no clocks ticking away the hours. It is possible that your guide may have lived on earth hundreds of years ago or even longer. Your guide was a real person not a fictional character. They were flesh and blood.

For example, the Native American Indians behind this book would have roamed the prairies long before the white man arrived. Another guide, Jimmy, will introduce himself shortly. He died of his wounds in the First World War, at the Battle of Ypres in 1917.

When a spirit on the other side of life chooses to become a guide they would have reached an advanced point in their spiritual development. Your guide would have a similar character and a natural empathy with you. It would be a like-for-like union. Their temperament and life experience would harmonise with yours. If you are in one of the caring professions as a nurse or doctor, then it is likely that your guide would have followed the same path. They would have been with you before you were born. They would have helped you prepare for this adventure on earth.

These words are from Black Feathers. He refers to souls on earth as Mediums. This is because spirit considers any person who conducts themselves in a way that reflects spiritual values, as representing them as Mediums in the widest sense. This is not quite the same as Mediums who are trained, dedicated and actively work for spirit. We'll come on to that shortly, for now this is Black Feathers talking:

"The role of the Guide is one of love and friendship, they are there to help, mentor and protect. They will never judge, they would never take their chosen Medium down a road of which they would be uncomfortable. They would never fill their Medium's thoughts with ego or with thoughts that would cause harm to others. They are your friends; the bonding of a friendship lasts until the two energies meet back in our world. They would never let you down, even if the Medium would become disheartened with the development between the two energies, which is natural. On your earth, time is of importance; people want things to happen quickly. When the process is slow it can cause frustration on the earth's side, but the guide will still be there at your side with an abundance of love and patience.

The guide would have taken many years to harmonise and get to know the energies with whom they are working and have to take into account the personality, life-style, setbacks and traumas that a Medium would face. It is the role of the guide to be able to know when the time is right for that person to develop the gifts that they have been given, in order for it to be the right time for them to progress. No guide would push to the extent that it would cause mental or physical harm to their Medium.

Guides do not control their Mediums. It is a partnership of pure love and friendship. The entwining of energies can work as one and be the best friend that would never let you down. This is natural in your world; the guides understand for they have also at one point been in an earthly existence. They have chosen this role. They are spirit messengers whose only aim is to help disperse the love and light from our world to yours."

## Knowing your guide

Becoming more spiritually aware and being more sensitive to the energies you detect from Spirit will help you to link with your guide. Becoming more aware is a process that often begins with meditation and of learning how to connect with Spirit. Blending energies with your guide takes time. It is a process of developing trust and understanding. The closer you become, the greater your spiritual talents will blossom. We'll explain more about raising energies and connecting with spirit in Chapter Four.

Talk to your guide in your head, or out-loud if you prefer. It is important to reach out and invite them into your life. They are waiting for your conscious invitation. How will you know when they've accepted your invitation? They will leave a subtle sign, their 'calling card'. When you reach a point of stillness in your mind and are free from the disturbances of the day, you may sense a velvet touch to your cheek or a gentle lightness of air around your ears, or feel a deft twist of hair, or a light tickle on your scalp. When this happens, they are with you. Believe in them. Trust in them. They will send a signal. This may not happen immediately; you have to work to create the connection.

You may have noticed references to the senses and sensory stimulus. We must value them, treasure them. An experienced guide pointed out that they have a sensory memory of all feelings, taste, touch, smell and physical sensations like heat and freezing cold, of every single emotion and excitement. They are locked in their minds. When they connect with us they can recapture those feelings but we should never take them for granted, as we are experiencing them in reality. Eventually, we will return to spirit and have them locked in our minds as memories.

## Call upon your support team of guides

During your lifetime, your main guide will be joined by another group of supporters. They will be other experienced guides who are specialists on issues that confront you. It's as if they are called in to give you extra help and advice on emotional or material or spiritual issues that occur at different points in your life. All you need to do is to think of spirit and ask them to come to your aid. Believe in them and they will be there with you to lighten your load. They in turn will be assisted by helpers who are spirits that are training to become guides. These helpers will contribute what they have learned during their lifetimes on earth. It is like having a rapid response team ready when needed. They could help on building confidence and strength if you're being bullied or are lacking self-confidence. Or, your support team could give extra love and encouragement during relationship stress. Speak to them in your mind. They are there for you. You can sometimes sense them in your sleep state.

Running Water sent Janet this message on the theme of spirit guides. It stresses the close bond between you and your spirit guide. It is a lifelong partnership of love and trust. This message arrived in Janet's mind as a jumble of letters. As she types, the letters take the form of sentences and paragraphs, like a jigsaw puzzle of letters.

"From the moment of your birth there are people around you nurturing and teaching you how to walk, talk and to find your own place within the world where you find yourself living. Through the passages of time you each go through different stages of your life. They are broken down into sections being new born to a small child, the older child into adolescence, the young adult then the adult. Through each of these stages you will meet many people. Some of these people will be there to help, guide and influence you for your life's journey. They may only be in your life for a short time but the knowledge and education they have given you will be invaluable to you and will help you from stage to stage of your life. You will make many friends, some will stay by your side and others will move on. Each one would have left you with memories, some you may wish to forget and other memories that will be of great help to you on your forward journey. These are people in a physical form that you can touch, see and speak with. This feels natural to you because you are all living beings, existing in a physical world.

It is also natural that you take some of the information and guidance for granted as you grow and advance in knowledge. You only see it as developing your life's journey and fail to see it as life's lesson and a guiding light. At times, people can also hinder you; this is a valuable lesson. It's to teach you patience and compassion; and how to think things for yourself. Go back to childhood: you are taught in school the necessary lessons for your adult life. You are given the information and questions; but have to arrive at your own answers. The care you take in the teaching is so you can learn and walk forward. There will be times when you fail to connect with someone and the learning will become non-existent. At these times you will seek and search until you find the right pathway.

You are living in a material world where negativity is playing a major role, thus influencing the outcome of much of the learning that you are receiving. This negativity takes away from the peace and tranquility which is much needed in your lives.

When people of your world find themselves connecting with the spiritual energies it's only natural that they become inquisitive of whose energy is surrounding them, to help guide them along their spiritual journey. Once that journey begins then it becomes like a replica of your physical life, except the Helpers and Guides who come and go throughout your journey are pure of spirit with only love and peace the first thought of the mind.

We then become your friends who only have the best of intentions; and that is to help and guide you on your spiritual journey. We are there to guide and help. Your role is to allow our energies to blend with your energies, to be fine-tuned, where we can work together as one. How you achieve this depends on how much dedication and discipline and attentiveness you put in. If you run before you can walk, then you will fall at the first hurdle. With time and patience you will be rewarded with the fulfilment of a lasting relationship with your spiritual friends. It's important for the Medium to understand that there is always the one main guide, or energy, there with them, shining the guiding light of Spirit from birth to the return to spirit. In between those times, there will be many more energies in the form of Helpers and Guides to help out at certain times of your life. Each time you are ready to walk forward onto another path there will be a new helper there to direct you in the right direction. As it was mentioned, it is a joint effort between the Medium and their guides. We become a partnership, working and blending together to help forward information and love from Spirit.

There may be times when your material life will interfere with the development of your spiritual path. At times such as these, by drawing our energies close we will be there to help you through such trials. We cannot interfere with your material lives they are there for you to find your own way through. We are there to help by giving you the comfort only our spiritual energies can provide."

It's interesting to think that your personal guide never stops learning and developing. We are all on the same path of enlightenment; only at different points on the same mission. Your guide has their helpers, their guides, their teachers too. It's a constant cycle of learning with higher guides and very highly evolved guides passing their knowledge onward. This lifetime contains pages from your spiritual history. As each page turns you become more complete.

## Guardian Angels

Guides were flesh and blood. Your guardian angel is a light being of pure celestial energy. Angels surround us. They form a protective layer against negative energies generated on earth. You know yourself when you witness anger and hatred first-hand or when you hear about atrocities committed during wars; or when elephants and other wildlife are slaughtered. Your senses recoil. That negative energy is a power that rises in the atmosphere. Angels within the world of spirit are a potent defence against it. They provide protection. Their love cleanses and washes away harm.

Angels are active on earth. You may have heard stories of people being pulled back onto the pavement out of the way of an oncoming car, or someone feeling a wind from nowhere, or hearing a warning shout that stops them in their tracks to avoid a calamity. I only mention it because someone, who I know and trust, experienced an earth-angel for real. His car had broken down on a snowy, icy road in the middle of nowhere. His head was inside the engine space trying to sort out the problem and repeatedly failing, when a man asked if he needed any help. The man told my friend to get behind the wheel and turn the ignition key. The engine coughed spluttered and started. Full of thanks my friend got out the car. There was no sign of the rescuer, no sound of a car driving away, no tracks in the snow. When he thought about it, he didn't hear a car arrive either. The road was completely deserted. Angels do adopt the human form and walk amongst us, sometimes as the poorest people with the greatest kindness, to provide a helping hand.

Do Angels have wings? For many years artists have depicted them with a magnificent pair of wings that sweep away evil and transport them with a silent swish of night air to be with you. If you want them to have wings, they will have wings. Angels are helpers. Children believe in them. As we grow older we should not forget them. In Chapter Five we'll introduce you to more guides and provide examples of the vital working relationship between us.

## Coming Next:

Mediums are messengers of evidence. Chapter Three explains how they work and how you too can learn the skills of mediumship over time. The difference between Spiritual and Psychic Mediums will be explained along with spiritual healing, a priceless gift of giving from Mediums.

# CHAPTER THREE

# Spiritual Mediumship

What's the difference between a Psychic Medium and a Spiritual Medium?

Psychics or Psychic Mediums have developed the psychic gifts of intuition to a point where they can read someone's aura to get a sense of their mental state of mind, the state of health, or the general way they are feeling. Over time, they have learned to accurately assess personality and character traits. By physical contact, touching hands for example, psychics can draw more information about a person at a particular moment in time. The way people speak, dress and sensing their moods are all indictors of their current material or emotional situation. Broadly speaking, psychics use their natural, intuitive skills, sometimes aided by tarot cards, astrology or other tools, to provide information on matters relating to our personal lives, romance, finances and career prospects, for instance, Psychic Mediums concentrate on the here-and-now aspects of your material life, using their intuition to build a mental image of the person sitting with them.

They can use their psychic talents from the same Four Gifts of Intuition as the Spiritual Medium. This results in being able to read a person by giving them advice in their relationships, career or whatever else is important to that person at that particular time. It is also possible that they can mention a loved one who has passed. This is because the deceased person will still be very much in the mind of the person receiving the message.

Psychic Mediums can play an important part in many people's lives, especially if someone has an important decision to make and find that they need advice from an independent agent. It's up to the receiver if they want to follow the advice given. But many times the receiver will get the answer to what they are looking for by making up their own minds, using only some of the information they have been given. In a loose way, it's like fortune telling. The danger is that it's a common occurrence where people will try to make the information fit to their liking or way of thinking; therefore leading them onto a completely different pathway. The psychic is not connecting to the spiritual energies, they are just engaging with their own psychic abilities and also the reliance of the receiver's interaction; that is, the feedback or information on why they want advice. For some people, a psychic can be a comfort blanket to be there when needed.

Some Mediums will combine the two different ways of working especially if they are finding it difficult to connect with an energy for the sitter, so therefore, they will connect with the person's aura to give a reading that way. But that is not a spiritual reading.

The key point of difference between them is that while they both have psychic talents, it's the way these talents are used that distinguishes them. Spiritual Mediums are so called because they use their talents for spiritual purposes. They provide evidence to prove the existence of the spirit world. Using their clairvoyance skills, they connect with friends and family that have passed. Close personal messages are given with only you in mind.

A Spiritual Medium's talents would involve all Four Gifts of Intuition when passing on a message from spirit. At any one time they may be leading with Clairvoyance (seeing) but call upon Clairsentience (feeling), Clairaudience (hearing) and Claircognisence (knowing) to provide a fully comprehensive picture for the person receiving the message from the spirit world. This is to reaffirm the link with departed spirits and the existence and influence of the spirit world. We've said that everyone has the potential to develop the spiritual gifts they were born with. Spiritual Mediums would develop their skills over time; for them it is a calling.

Novice Mediums need to blend their energies with their spirit guides. This can take years and cannot be rushed. The blending is for the two parties to tune-in. Their thought energies would be like getting a strong, crackle-free radio signal when searching for the right station. The two points of communication must be in-sync. When a Spiritual Medium concentrates and directs their thought energies to their guide the two energies become one. The guide would have been looking after their Medium since birth. We all have our own principle guide as we all have our own guardian angel. Spirit guides would have reached a high level of training themselves before they are given the responsibility of looking after a Medium on earth. Developing their psychic skills needs to go hand in hand with Mediums having tuition in delivering messages. A Medium must have empathy with the recipient when passing on highly sensitive information and must also appreciate the impact it can have. This underlines the vocational nature of their work as ambassadors of Spirit and their duty to others.

## Clairvoyant evidence of everlasting life

The primary duty of a Spiritual Medium is to prove that life continues after death. It is their duty to pass on the love from friends and family who are no longer here. However, their spirit still lives. They may not be in the material world but they still exist in mind, thought and energy. The moment you think of a loved one, they come alive. How can someone who you don't know provide the kind of proof your heart yearns for? What kind of evidence can they supply to convince you? What will it take for you to feel that divine surge of understanding and experience that sublime revelation?

We all have psychic ability. It stems from your psyche or brain. It is that invisible source of deepest thought energy from our minds. Many of us never tap into this ability. It lays dormant, undiscovered. Often the only hint we have is when our intuition triggers an idea in our heads or we get a twinge in our gut. A Spiritual Medium has often gone through years of training to accept, embrace and link their spirituality together with their spirit guide.

The process connects our two worlds; it is a blending of mind energy. Simply put, the Medium performs the role of communicator, the go-between. They accept and direct messages from Spirit. Spirit makes contact when they want to speak to us. A Medium cannot decide to make contact as if they are making a person-to-person call. Spirit control the communication exchange, they make the first move. Deceased spirits make contact with the spirit guide, using their thought energy, when they want to pass on a message.

This is when the earth contact is made. Imagine a church service and you are a member of the congregation. Spirit cannot see matter. We each have our own spiritual light that emanates from our aura and shines from the top of our heads. The brighter the light the more spiritually aware you are. The Medium senses or sees your light in their minds. The role of the Medium is to firstly identify the deceased spirit-side who wants to communicate with someone in the congregation.

Often the sequence begins with the Medium saying of what relation, friend or family they are to you. This may be followed by a physical description of the departed spirit when they were living here. The clothes they wore, the way they walked, their height and weight, perhaps their name. More information follows, perhaps about their personality, the type of person they were and how you interacted with them. As this information flows, the Medium will check with you to see if you recognise the person from Spirit. They will want to hear your voice as this is important to create and maintain contact across the ether.

When you realise who has 'come through', a personal message is usually given. The message concerns your spiritual self. It is about aspects of your life to prove that they know you, and want to send love and guidance that really resonates. In a public meeting Janet's guide follows three golden rules. These are, to never embarrass, never to give your personal business away and never to give bad news.

Clairvoyance provides evidence. Your loved ones who have passed are still alive in spirit. Watching over and caring for you. Think of them as your extended family on the other side of life. A Spiritual Medium can give comfort and put people's minds at rest by making a connection to a departed spirit. This can sometimes be done very quickly after a person has passed over into spirit.

The departed spirit must want to make contact. Spirit contact us. Not the other way round. They are not on speed-dial waiting for us to ring. It is their decision to link with loved ones.

## Janet's Clairvoyant Messages

"To be a Medium is a privilege. To receive a communication from spirit and to pass that message on is a gift I cherish."

When spirits communicate, loved ones can pass on proof of continuing life with small personal touches that mean the world or address issues left unresolved before passing. Here are some examples of clairvoyant memories told by Janet and some remembered by those who received the message:

A Small Boy's Message to his Mother recalled by Janet:

"A few years ago a young couple came to me for a sitting. Halfway through, I felt that a small child was with me. Their son wanted them to know he was alright. I found out a few weeks later that he was their three year old who had died of Leukaemia.

After that the mother often came to see me and her son always comes through. He is such a lovely energy. He would say how he loved sleeping with his Nan and he always bought his favourite toy car with him. Of all the energies I have had, I would say he is the loveliest. He told his mum he was going to have a new brother; which she did about two years later. He would bring so much love and happiness with him."

## Sue's Story:

"My dad came through ten years ago and told me that there were three babies due in the family. I soon found out my son and girlfriend were expecting. And that my niece and nephew respectively were aslo expecting. But my father told me I wouldn't be happy.I was confused and didn't understand. I would have been happy whatever the situation. I wracked my brains thinking of every scenario.

He was right. On the same day my niece gave birth to a boy. My nephew had a girl. Sadly we lost our first grandchild. I then understood."

## Mark's Memories

"I am lucky to know Janet as a family friend, and, since meeting her many years ago, I have learned more about her gift. I was a little apprehensive before the first sitting, having no idea of what to expect. It was done in such a natural manner, not theatrical or anything like that, just sitting listening to Janet passing on messages from patients who wanted to express their gratitude for my care. To explain, I am a nurse and have worked in Palliative Care for many years.

She also relayed to me a scene which has been a feature in my dreams for as long as I can remember. It was of me in a rowing boat on the water, under a pier. From the pier supports were hanging lines of different coloured Chinese lanterns, lighting up the dark and reflecting on the ripples of the water as the boat made its way. It was such a specific image that I hadn't mentioned to anyone but it was such a comforting feeling to hear Janet describe this scene so accurately.

There was another occasion when Janet said "Did your Dad used to do this?" She made a thumbs-up signal but the way she did it was kind of pointing down and in a funny punching action. I was so taken aback because that was exactly what he used to do in a 'well done' or 'good for you' sort of way. I can see him do it now as I describe it. Janet told me that my Dad was there and just wanted to say how happy he was that I was keeping well. I was so pleased to be told that. It was such a strange out of the blue experience, but very much my Dad, as a memory of a really special time it makes me feel very emotional and warm to think of that experience."

## Jane's Reconciliation

"I've known Janet for some time now and we've become firm friends. I've had readings from other Mediums in the past but Janet made me feel relaxed as we got to know each other. She provided accurate descriptions of people and got their personalities perfectly, there was no doubt who was speaking. In fact, speaking to the spirit of my mother was the gateway to our gradual reconciliation. There was a family breakup when my brother and I were very young. She asks forgiveness with every reading. Healing can continue after someone passes away."

Safe and Happy – Reassuring Messages from Loved Ones recalled by Janet:

"People come to me when they have lost a partner. If they've been together for a very long time, the remaining partner can often find it very hard to cope with the loss and move on. When this happens, the partner who has passed tries to come through as soon as they can. This could be as quickly as only a week since their passing. They provide a lot of identifying evidence to pass on to give comfort and certainty. All the remaining partner wants to know is that their loved one is safe and happy and any pain or illness they had has gone."

### Father and Son Reunion – Janet tells the story:

Recently, I was approached by a gentleman who had been given my details for a reading over the phone. This was during the pandemic caused by the Coronavirus when I could not hold person-to-person meetings. He was a complete stranger and had never had a reading from a Medium before. As soon as I connected with Spirit, an energy came through to say he was the father of the man on the call. The father described in detail how poorly he was and how much he suffered towards the end of his life. He continued communicating, allowing his lively personality to shine through.

The accurate information was great evidence that it was his father. The son knew in an instant that it was his father's energy that was contacting him to assure the rest of the family that he was happy in spirit and feeling no pain.

His father continued to explain how he had chosen the wrong time to pass: his family had been denied a proper funeral. Because of social distancing, only ten people were allowed to attend a funeral. He continued to say how much he was looking forward to holding a proper wake when many friends and family could have a good old time.

Afterwards, his son told me his father had died five weeks before and they couldn't have a proper funeral; but the family would have a memorial for him once lockdown is over and it will involve a really big 'do'.

The gratitude and joy from the son on receiving this information was something that made me feel I'd done my job. And, that Spirit were using my energies to make this happen. I saw the son the following day to pass over a recording of the meeting. The look of relief and happiness on his face and the words of appreciation is something that will stay in my memory for years to come.

That's what mediumship is all about; being able to provide proof that a loved one is able to make contact, and to give assurance that they are very much alive in spirit."

## Healing Energies

Spiritual healing is the channeling of energy from the universe. A healing Medium acts as the conduit to channel the magnetic power of Spirit, for the benefit of a recipient. In your mind's eye, you could visualise it as a beam of light being directed to soothe, relax and rebalance the body, mind and spirit. Spiritual healing complements and is not an alternative to conventional medicine. The two modes of healing often work together by the de-stressing and comforting effect of spirit aiding the medical advice and recovery process. The body is relaxed, tensions are eased and self-healing is stimulated.

Kindness, compassion and caring are all part of the healing spectrum. You shine your spiritual light when helping, sharing and supporting others. A simple smile, a kind word, taking a moment to be silent and listen to someone 'off-load' their worries and concerns is an underrated but potent spiritual tonic you can dispense.

Caring can be channelled physically through the laying on of hands. By having the intention of healing you can channel energy from Spirit through your hands and on to the point of pain. This could be either a physical discomfort or mental stress. The recipient may feel the warmth generated to relax and rebalance the mind, body and spirit. As mentioned before, this is an example of the power of thought, coupled with the intention to heal, that draws the energy from Spirit. The mind is a magnet for spiritual energy.

This mental energy can be transferred by thought to a person who is not physically present. This is termed as absent or distant healing. By engaging the power of thought, the healer can transmit healing energies to wherever the recipient may be. There is a strict code of conduct for healers to follow. Spiritual healing cannot claim to cure a medical or mental illness. The main benefit lies in a person entering a more relaxed state that helps the mind and body to heal itself. Spiritual healing can benefit someone, whether the person receiving the healing believes in the process or not. Reiki is another healing practice of Japanese and Chinese origin that uses direct hands-on-body or palm healing.

These words are from White Bear a highly regarded healing guide:

"The power of healing can be given through many different avenues. The most common form of healing is the laying on of hands or touching the aura or energy field. Absent healing and distant healing are both just as effective in a way, although most feel the benefit more from the healer being present.

Healing can also be given by the listening ear. Some people feel they would rather talk to someone, who will listen to them. It is a caring therapy to be able to talk to someone knowing that they are listening and not interrupting. Another method can be by just sitting with someone holding their hand in the silence. Words are not always needed in fact they can be disruptive at times.

When healing is taking place, the healer becomes a conduit for spiritual energy. The energy from the guide is then transferred to the healer's energy which, in turn, is transmitted onto the energy field of the person or animal who is receiving the healing. How much strength is in the energy varies from healer to healer. You also have to take into account the physical or mental condition of the sitter.

Spiritual healing is not a cure for all ills. It has never been claimed that spirit can completely heal all illnesses or diseases. It is used for comfort and the relief of many distresses which are caused by illness or one of the many problems people face in their lifetime. You can compare it to a non-invasive therapy which can calm the mind and the spiritual being.

There have been many stories in your world where people have claimed to have received healing to find they have been cleared of illnesses where they thought there was no cure. These, my friend, have not been coincidental occurrences. The body at times can cure itself but the healing energy would certainly have helped by relieving stress around that person."

We all have the potential to direct healing energies to those in need. Purely by being present, and listening to someone as they share their pain, can ease mental anguish. The elderly and lonely can be deprived of any form of human contact for days or weeks on end. The simple warmth of smiling can deliver care to another human being. It is Spirit making the contact.

## Channelling – Another method of spirit communication

Bit by bit, step by gentle step, channelling opens the world of Spirit to us. It is another way of communicating with a world that wants to share love and knowledge. Channelling is a two way stream of information. It can take the form of words flowing into the mind of the Medium, to be written down rather than being spoken out loud. These are words of introduction from Jimmy, a guide who was a soldier in the First World War. He died of his wounds in Ypres Belgium in 1917. We'll let Jimmy take over. Janet channelled this message and wrote it down for you enjoy.

"My dear friend, it is a pleasure to be able to place words on paper that will only be there to help you and make you smile.

It seems that we have now had permission to be able to communicate to you through the written word. This is to be done with much care and attention from our world and we are not to get carried away thinking we can communicate every other day. We are pleased though, now the rule has been lifted, to enable our energies to feel free to express any words we might think you would like to read.

Where shall I start? The beginning is always the best place to start, that way any future letters will just be a continuation of the last one.

I found myself covered in dust and rubble with wounds all over my body. There had been a lot of noise from the artillery attack from the opposite side. It's a nasty business war, one always has to ask themselves why can't the politicians ever come to an agreement that will save lives and not destroy them? But, there again, there is always that one person who wants to rule the world. I would just prefer to stay at home and go to the pub on a Sunday lunchtime rather than take control of the whole damn world. Before the war started, we would sit and listen to what was going on between the politicians and the Kaiser, the mad man over in Germany. We all knew it was coming-that is, anyone with an ounce of sense did. Some people blocked it out of their minds because they were still recovering from the last one in Africa with the Boer War. The whole world at war with one another, what a waste of time, but, then again, we have to fight for our country to protect the innocent.

I was just a soldier like any other man fighting to protect one and all. 'It's a duty for the country' is what we were forever hearing from the people sitting smugly behind their desks, well away from any harm, safe within their bunkers. Not that I, for one minute, would have preferred to be with them. No fear! My place was out there amongst it all. We all knew that only half would return home at the end of it. Fear is something that only spurs you on in those circumstances. Fear is what we place within our own minds: we put it there, no-one else does. We all worked as one trying to defeat and not be defeated. It was a bloody affair in more ways than one. To see the life of your friend taken in a second is a shock, but in those circumstances, you would just thank the Lord it was them and not you at that particular time. We didn't have the time to grieve. That would have to wait until we got home, that's if we ever did. Some did. I didn't. My remains are buried somewhere out there in France. There were far too many bodies to bring back home so, instead, we were placed in the ground not far from where we had fallen.

The life didn't ebb away from me instantly; no, I didn't have that luxury. Instead, gangrene set in and, within a few days or a week, and after a lot of pain, I eventually saw the light. What a strange thing to even think about; the light. What did I expect? A person walking in front of me holding a lighted match? No. I felt lighter in myself and everything around me went quiet and peaceful, then there was the light. You don't see it with your eyes because you don't have them anymore. It's just light.

Of course, news soon found its way over to the family and to the wife. It was the telegram they feared; they only ever brought bad news, never good. But so many of us were taken that news of yet another death was becoming all too common. This is just a short narrative of how I arrived here. Not for any sympathy; we don't want that once we have arrived. Sympathy is something that is kept solely for the earth. We don't need it here. Once here, it's us who have sympathy for you all left on the earth.

You might be wondering, at this point, what my role is now. You must be thinking to yourself 'surely he has a role or why else would he be communicating?' My role is yet to be revealed. One step at a time, there is no need to rush things.

So here I find myself. It's strange isn't it? I'm still referring to myself as a person but then you know that it's only a figure of speech, like being able to communicate with the physical 'you'. Don't expect too much from me at the moment. 'One step at a time' is my motto. We all work together as a team; that would be the army training still within me. Slowly and steadily, we will tread along the golden path of knowledge. It's here that I feel a confession is forthcoming and that is that knowledge for certain subjects has always escaped me but for common sense and trivial information, you can always count on Jimmy!

That's my name or it was my given name from birth. I apologise for not introducing myself at the beginning of this note but then as I said I am very new to this form of communication. I think it's here that the conversation will come to an end for the time being. This is a very useful way of making contact. It's more of a personal note. When we converse, it's more open for everyone else to listen, which at those times, is when interference starts to creep into the conversations. We have to take into account the personalities and ability of the others present to be able to grasp what is being said, plus we have to give way to the others who are waiting to speak.

The gong has gone now; it's time for me to depart. Don't worry if you do not hear from me for a while, it's the queueing system you see. We all take our turn and all that, plus we have all been informed that you have a lot of work to continue with for your next book. As I said we all have to give way to others.

Cheerio for now, Jimmy.

We felt it was important for you to have the chance to read all one thousand, one hundred words of Jimmy's message. The words ring true on so many levels. His rage at the establishment running the war, his call of duty, and making the ultimate sacrifice, touched the heart. It also opened a window to the spirit world and provided a wonderful example of how both worlds communicate on a human level of emotional understanding.

## Direct Channeling by Voice

It can take years of trust and dedication for the energies of both Medium and guide to reach a level where they blend seamlessly. This is so that the denser, heavier energy of the earthbound Medium can flow beautifully between the lighter, higher energy of the spirit guide. When this is achieved, the channeling can move from a written to a higher level. The thoughts and messages of the guide can be spoken using the Medium's vocal cords. This is a harmonious interaction by both parties. Guide and Medium connect using mind-to-mind thought energy. In some cases, Mediums can be aware of the words being said by their guide fractionally before they are spoken out loud. If the mental interaction goes deeper, the Medium may not sense what is being said as they speak.

Like any conversation, the guide and Medium need someone to talk to. Spirit likes to hear a human voice in response, to complete the circle of communication. It gives great joy for a spirit to know their words are making an impact on physical beings on earth. In most cases, this direct communication begins with the primary guide of the Medium starting the meeting. The guide may introduce themselves by name, or with prompting, can be encouraged to identify themselves. Every relationship between Medium and guide is special. Some Mediums will work with only one guide. Others will be joined by guides from the higher realms or ones that have a particular interest in the subject under discussion.

The topic can be anything under the sun. Once the meeting has begun, other guides with the approval of the main guide, may also speak. The convention is for highly evolved guides to use their seniority to join the conversation and make their contribution when they choose. As you would expect, the energy levels required to support this direct communication is intense. The lighter the energy results in the Medium's voice sounding as they usually do, but the words spoken may have an inspirational flavour, as they are from spirit. If the energy level is deeper and denser, the voice and personality of the communicating guide will be more evident in the delivery.

A deeper, altered state of awareness is often described as Trance Mediumship where a Medium is entranced by Spirit. The dictionary gives a definition of entranced as: 'to fill (someone) with wonder and delight while holding their entire attention.' This is where their guide speaks through them using the Medium's vocal chords. Spirit is hugely protective of their Mediums and would not subject anyone to this deeper level unless they were physically strong and mentally willing to participate. Also, the relationship between guide and Medium would have produced a solid bond of trust between them. As this relationship is so deep it often involves a spirit guide working with their one particular Medium. In Janet's case, she works with Running Water in a slightly different way. Rather than going deep with one guide, Running Water acts as a doorkeeper and allows different spiritual energies to visit and pass on their thoughts and messages through her.

## The Monday Night Channeling Circle

On Monday night, Janet hosts her channeling or trance circle. It is held in her front room with curtains closed, and flickering candles create a calm relaxed atmosphere. It is a teaching circle where Mediums of advanced experience are invited to develop their blending and relationship skills with spirit. Each meeting is opened and closed with a prayer of love and respect. That's where I come in. I'm not clairvoyant. My role is to keep a watchful eye while the Mediums enter a state of entrancement. When the Mediums start working with their guides I make sure they are not disturbed by anyone entering the room. The energies in the room are hypersensitive and should not be disturbed by phones ringing or other possible distractions. This is a precious time creating a sacred connection with Spirit.

Cindy and Suzi are part of the circle with Janet. Both are talented Mediums who have had years of training to reach this point. Before the meeting begins, the three agree the order of contact with their primary guide. With Cindy it would be Adam. With Suzi it would be Alun. Running Water usually opens the session with Janet. There is no set time for the meeting to run for. That's in the hands of Spirit. It used to be around the hour mark but recently the activity is so busy, with many energies visiting, it has lasted for up to eighty minutes. The meeting flows, with each Medium sometimes speaking to three or more energies each. They fade-in and fade-out when they've delivered their contribution. Spirit love to talk. They enjoy hearing their words being spoken out loud on earth and for their ideas, lessons and guidance to be passed from a spiritual energy to a human mind.

This is how Janet describes connecting with Spirit:

"After the opening prayer, I close my eyes and mentally hand over my thoughts to the spiritual energies that work with me. It immediately feels like a subtle change in the energies that surround me. It's as if they've placed a thin, white cloak over my material mind to separate it from the spiritual work that's about to begin. The effect of this is that the room and surroundings are set to one side as my conscious thoughts take a back seat. I'm still aware of what's happening in the room but, for now, it seems slightly distant as the spiritual energies increase. The change is my signal to prepare for their presence.

About half a second before they converse, I become aware of whose energy is with me. I recognise them by their personality and by the strength of their energy. The feeling is like having surging waves flowing over and through me, some stronger than others. It all depends on how advanced is the visiting energy. The most powerful are advanced spirits from the higher realms. Their power descends from these lighter, purer levels towards our lower, denser, energies that are closer to earth's atmosphere.

Running Water has a gentle energy. We have been together for many years, with him as my mentor and friend. Every meeting carries its own purpose. They are not all serious. Sometimes a smile will come across my face when I sense that spirits with a great sense of humour are about to speak. This is always with the Scribe and also Charlie; they are the two who bring a sense of humour. Josiah's energy is like that of frenzied excitement, he can't contain himself. With the others, as I said, it's like different waves blending in and out. Because I have been doing it for such a long time I nearly always know who they are as many have become old friends. When a spirit has finished speaking they fade their energies in farewell to leave space for a fresh energy to swell and join the conversation. In case you're wondering, there is a sense of physical tiredness after a long session; but it's not exhausting, as spirit direct their energies through my etheric body and not directly through my mortal body.

This is an excerpt from a recorded conversation with Running Water. We were talking about how we like to know the name of the guides who visit us; to help identify them by their personality. Running Water explained how Native American Indian babies were named at their birth according to the natural elements that were at play when they came into the world. Running Water spoke using Janet's vocal cords:

"Babies were named after the land, the moon, the stars or animals or from where they were born. I was born near a stream. My precious grand-daughter was born by a river at night, where the reflection of a full moon was rippling on the wavelets. Her name is 'Moondance'. There's always a reason why a name was inspired by nature. This includes names like Sunrise, Rising Moon, Golden Eagle, Lone Wolf and Grey Dove. Spirit influences are everything to us - the land, the rocks, the plants, the air; absolutely everything in creation. We praised the spirit of every animal we killed and we used each part of the animal. We depended upon each other.

This message on the subject of written and verbal communication is from a high guide known as 'Scribe', who is an supremely evolved teaching guide in The Halls of Learning.

"There are many words that we can write to you or utter to you, it all depends upon the subject of which we wish to refer to at the time. There are many thoughts going around in your head and it is with these thoughts how the conversations will go.

It is not only through the written word and the verbal conversations that we can contact you. Our energies are very much now implanted within your own energy field, which allows us to be able to give you the guidance of which you seek.

Once you have the faith and beliefs firmly implanted within your mind then it becomes easier for us to commence with the blending of our energies. You are noticing subtle changes around your own persona. How you are finding the ability to be able to diffuse certain situations, where in previous times you would have failed to do so, consequently making matters worse. You are becoming more patient and are looking at the broader picture. Certain things in your life now are becoming of no consequence whereas before they would seem important. This is how we are working with you. Flexibility, my friend, allows the mind not only to be able to link into how we work but will also allow yourself to think on your own feet at a moment's notice and to be prepared for any events that will come your way, whether they be spiritual or material.

It was felt that there was the need for us to impart with this information for your own benefit. Clarity will overcome doubts within your mind.

All the various guides you have spoken with all come with different attributes. Each and every one of us works with you in different ways. Do not make the mistake by thinking we are only there so you can pass information onto others. My energy is there for you, my friend, so you can finally know who you are and what your purpose is for the future.

I leave these words with you, my friend. The Scribe"

## A Medium's Viewpoint

We thought it would be interesting to give you an insight into what a clairvoyant Medium would be thinking as they prepare to receive, then pass on, a message from Spirit to you.

A spiritual Medium must faithfully represent the words of Spirit when giving a message, sometimes called a 'reading'. It's a term for the information being passed from Spirit via the Medium to the sitter. The word 'sitter' is used to describe the person receiving the message. It's a personal and sensitive exchange. The nature of the delivery may change depending on whether it is a private, one-to-one meeting or during a public service. In a spiritualist church, Mediums work on a raised platform in front of the congregation. What is said in a private meeting can be more in-depth but in public Mediums have to be particularly mindful of people's privacy.

These are points a Medium could consider when passing on information from Spirit to the recipient;

1. Give what you get: Don't let your normal questioning mind interfere or misinterpret the information you receive as a Medium from Spirit. Something may sound silly to you but it could be the thing that resonates with the sitter. It may make perfect sense to them.

2. Avoid asking questions of the sitter: Spiritual Mediums communicate directly with spirit guides so any questions should be put to spirit using a thought/mind connection. Mediums can ask for confirmation from the sitter that what has been said is correct, or to check whether what has been

said has been properly understood. They should avoid being fed information by the sitter. This is often difficult because people want to help.

3. Hear the sitter's voice clearly: When a Medium is directed at a particular person, it is common for them to be shy or slightly embarrassed to be chosen by the Medium, and surprised at becoming the centre of attention. They nod their head instead of answering with a clear 'yes' or 'no'. Spirit do not 'see' physical bodies they sense a person's light that emanates from their aura, and they hear the sound of their voice. That's why it's so important for the sitter to speak clearly.

4. Don't judge a sitter by their appearance: It's only natural to make snap judgements about someone by the way they look. A Medium needs to remove any personal prejudices when working.

5. Spirits are not fortune tellers. They will give information that people need for their spiritual life, but may not relate to their material lives. It is natural for people to ask about career, finance and emotional relationships but these elements are the area for psychic mediums who deal with earthly matters.

6. Be sensitive: Mediums, over years of training, learn how to soften news that could cause distress. This is especially true in church services held in public. A Medium will not deliberately say anything to cause upset, however readings are emotional by their very nature. Care has to be taken. Mediums must always

have in the forefront of their minds that departed spirits were greatly loved and are sorely missed.

7. Time to close down a message: Not everyone who attends a spiritual reading is open to the process. They may be cynical and doubt anything and everything. Sceptics, on the other hand, are people who demand evidence and strong argument but are generally prepared to accept convincing proof. If a Medium feels their channel of communication is blocked with profound negativity and the quality of the information from spirit is compromised, then it is best to close the sitting.

One thing Mediums should not forget…

Mediums are the voice of Spirit. They carry messages to enlighten and uplift. It is an immensely important role, at a time in someone's life when emotions are hyper-sensitive. Spirit put their trust in Mediums to use their power with care. Wang Chang warns of egos becoming distorted. Feeling pride in the gift a Medium has been given from Spirit is one thing. Basking in praise and adulation for personal recognition for an ego boost is not a good look.

## Coming Next:

We hope that each chapter will add more to your understanding of Spirit and your spirituality. Chapter Four will explain how to actively develop your spiritual talents. You will learn how to generate psychic energy and open your thoughts to what lies ahead.

CHAPTER FOUR

# Raising Energies and Connecting with Spirit

There are two other energy sources that make the spiritual 'you' so special. They are auras and chakras. These are two locations of spiritual energy in and around your body. Auras and chakras are complimentary energies that literally lift your spirits, the way you feel. They create a stairway to spiritual enlightenment.

Your aura comprises seven invisible energy layers that surround your *outer* body, like a multi-layered overcoat. Your chakras are centred *within* your body and create an imaginary vertical ladder of energy from your pelvis to the top of your head. The chakras transcend from the physical to the spiritual the higher they get. The highest chakra at the top of your head connects with the divine.

## Auras

The human body emits an aura. In fact, all living beings, birds, animals, plants, fish, insects emit an aura. It's an electro-magnetic field that surrounds your body, referred to as your auric field. In your mind's eye imagine it to be like the glow of vibrational energy that wraps around you. Auras have a spectrum of colours that reflect your personality and state of health. At times, auras change colour to suit a particular emotional and mental state; joyful or sad, healthy or ill. There are seven layers of aura colours. If you are bathed in the colour blue this will be healing energies at work from spirit. The higher the aura on a scale of one to seven the lighter, more refined and more spiritual they are.

This message from spirit is on the theme of auras:

"Spirit sees only lights. We do not see things in matter form. We only tune into the living energies. Any being with a beating heart that lives and breathes is what spirit recognises. It is the aura, the energy field around a living form, that attracts Spirit. There can be colours around the aura which tell of the person's situation in that particular time. Some can be green tinged with blue, some can be red of all different shades, different mauves also tinged with blue, some can be white and sparkling, some dull and cloudy, some can have the colours of the rainbow, layer upon layer. All these colours can give an experienced Medium an indication of how that person is coping with an emotional trauma, health issues, or problems involving their material world or general wellbeing."

## 7 Auric Layers surround our bodies

The auric layer surrounding and closest to our bodies is called the etheric layer. This is the most immediately reactive layer to the pressures and mental disturbances of our physical lives. When we want to calm down during meditation, or as we prepare to connect with Spirit, it is this layer that our thought energies will focus upon. Once this has been achieved a mental pathway lies before us to potentially reach the highest high. As we progress through the seven levels, we experience a finer, more sublime state of mind.

A spirit named Podano wanted to stress the importance of the Etheric body, and how it reacts within our aura. Think of the Etheric body as an invisible energy field enveloping our physical body. It is the light emitted from the Etheric layers that Spirit see. Spiritual energy flows to and from the Etheric body to the human mind. Spirit use the Etheric body as a preferred channel of communication, as it is composed of pure spiritual energy. When our physical bodies reach the end, our souls pass through the Etheric channel to the World of Spirit.

The Etheric layers wrap round your outer body in seven layers of energy. Your chakras are energy points located inside your body as shown in this chart

| Auric Level | Name | Outer Body Position | Representing | Aura Colour | Inner Chakra Position | Chakra Colour |
|---|---|---|---|---|---|---|
| 1st | Etheric | Closest to the body | The physical body | Bluish grey | Root Base Base of your spine | Red |
| 2nd | Emotional | Second from the body | Emotions & feelings | Can be all colours of the rainbow to reflect changing moods/health | Sacral/ pelvic area | Orange |
| 3rd | Mental | Third from the body | Thoughts & state of Mind | Bright Yellow | Solar Plexus | Yellow |
| 4th | Astral | Fourth from the body | Connection with the astral plane and mental travelling | Pink or Rose Coloured | Heart | Green |
| 5th | Etheric Template | Fifth from the body | Represents the body blueprint on this plane | Can vary in colour dependent on moods/health | Throat | Blue |
| 6th | Celestial | Sixth from the body | The link with the divine | Pearly white | Third Eye | Purple |
| 7th | Ketheric Template | Seventh the furthest layer away from the body | Feeling of being as one with the universe. Holds all the information about your soul & previous lifetimes | Gold | Crown Chakra | White |

## 7 Chakra Energy Positions from Base to Crown

## Connecting with spirit

Imagine a smile of deep satisfaction on your guide's face. You're about to connect with your greatest spiritual friend. It will take commitment and patience. It will take dedication, knowing that blending and progress could be a stop/start affair, as your material life is bound to throw a few curves in your path. The results can change your life, making you more confident and more in-tune with the world around you. It will open your mind to vistas you never thought possible.

Connecting with Spirit can begin in a very gentle way. It is appreciating the subtle difference between Spirit and spirituality. Spirituality is a code for living that reflects the way you are as a person. It is the essential 'you'. Being considerate, loving, kind, sharing, caring, thoughtful, doing unto others, being as one with nature, protecting this planet, offering a helping hand; these are all outward signs of your spirituality. These characteristics are ones that blend beautifully with exploring and absorbing knowledge of Spirit. As you've realised, spiritual growth never stops. It is a cycle of learnng and development over many incarnations and progress within the world of spirit. In the here and now, your process of growth can begin with visiting a spiritualist church and getting a feeling for the content of the services and courses on offer. You can experience a relaxed and welcoming atmosphere and watch the demonstrations of Mediumship. There's no pressure. You could also get a private reading from a Spiritual Medium. All the while, the accent is on providing evidence of the existence and role of Spirit in your life.

If you like what you see and feel and want to learn more, you could consider joining a learning Circle.

## Joining a spiritual learning circle

There are two types of Mediumship development Circle. One open, the other closed. Both are designed to help people explore and develop their spiritual gifts. An Open Circle, as the name suggests, is open to new members attending for a first time , or for those who are in the early stages who need flexibility in their attendance. A Closed Circle is for those who are ready to commit to a regular, structured, and progressive experience. Whatever stage you've reached, from knowing little and sensing little, to being able to tune-into spirit; everyone is seen as a spiritual equal. Equal in spirit but at different points in their development. An experienced Medium will chair the circle and manage the meeting. The meetings can be held anywhere that is conducive to creating a friendly and tranquil atmosphere in sympathetic surroundings.

## The meeting begins

Meetings are not rigid in structure and content but there are common elements. There are no textbooks or passages to read or homework to learn. The host Medium will shape the evening to suit the abilities of the membership. It will usually last between an hour and two hours. It is an opportunity to make new friends. After chatting and relaxing, the Medium may suggest an exercise to leave the stresses of the day outside the meeting for example:

## Blue Sky Preparation

This simple meditation was suggested by spirit. Visualisation is a great way to take your mind away from everyday pressures and concerns. Why don't you try it?

After calming yourself and sitting comfortably, with your feet flat on the floor and without shoes:

- Imagine an empty, bright blue sky.

- Slowly, a pure white cloud moves from the right of your vision and stops in the centre of the sky; in the middle of your forehead, in the 3$^{rd}$ eye position.

- Think about-then release- all the stresses and strains, irritations and distractions of the day, Take a moment to bring them front of mind, think about them and let them go.

- Mentally throw them into the cloud, like putting the rubbish out.

- The cloud will then move to the left and out of your vision. The blue sky returns. Take a breath and open your eyes.

## The Tree of Life -Part One

The tree of life is another meditation technique to help you steer the mind away from daily worries.

The tree of life is an ancient symbol of immortality. The roots intertwining with the branches of the tree create one continuous circle. They make the eternal connection between Heaven and Earth. The Tree of Life can be the inspiration for a powerful meditation exercise to raise the earth's magnetic force upward and draw down the Divine Light from above.

How about putting the book down for a moment and connecting with the tree of life? We think you'll enjoy it:

- To begin, sit comfortably in a chair so your feet, without shoes, can be flat on the floor. Rest your hands on your thighs. Gently roll your shoulders and move your head and neck from side to side to release any muscular tension.

- Close your eyes. Direct all your mental energy to your feet. Imagine you are as one with the earth. Visualise small tree roots sprouting from the soles of your feet and tiny roots stemming from your toes.

- See the roots burrow through the floor, driving down, piercing the foundations of your house, going deeper and deeper into the soil, past rocks and stones penetrating to the very centre of the earth.

- All the while, the roots are growing bigger and stronger drawing up earth's magnetic energy.

- Energy travels upwards through your roots like streams of molten lava. You look down. Your ankles, calves and legs have entwined to form the single trunk of the tree. Bark crackles and forms a protective layer as your tree trunk widens through your hips getting thicker and taller, going higher and higher, leaving the ground way below you.

- You look upwards. Your shoulders and arms have sprouted a thousand branches. Leaves have created a gloriously green canopy above you.

- You see a beam of dazzling light moving like a lightning strike through the canopy and down the trunk, to blend seamlessly with earth's magnetic energy rising upwards along your trunk to meet at your solar plexus, the heart centre of your being.

- Hold that image. Feel the spiritual energy pulse through your body. Stay in the moment for as long as you wish. Slowly open your eyes and come back.

## Sometimes it's not easy

Sometimes, despite trying hard, nothing happens. You could be waiting for that magical moment when the doors of enlightenment suddenly swing wide open, yet they stay firmly closed. This is what Chan, a revered teaching guide, said when I had the same problem:

"This is a problem with meditation. It is difficult for the mind to go blank. Everyone is different. You may have material issues that block the way. Energies blend with the energies around you. They are waiting for the slot to occur within your mind, but you are waiting for something magical to happen. This creates a barrier. If you can let your mind go so it is completely blank, a void, then there is no resistance, no issues to get in the way. Building this rapport takes time. Be calm, try to visualise a spiritual light in that void. Put your mind to one side. Sit on your own for a short five, ten or fifteen minutes and visualise the light. Discipline plays a part. Try to make this a regular experience and be consistent. Then you will begin to make progress and eventually connect with your energies."

Brown Bear wanted to give you some advice on connecting with spirit too:

"Don't be disheartened when trying to connect with Spirit. It will take time and, every time you try, the energies do get stronger. You don't have to think only of connecting to your one guide but to many guides who, together, create a mass of energy to welcome you. Imagine that thinking of one guide creates a film coating that wraps around your aura and that needs to be cleared away before we can penetrate. Don't force it by trying too hard to engage your mind. That creates a wall between us. Relax and disengage your brain. Put your mind to one side and we'll be there."

## The Opening Prayer

The Medium will ask everyone to extend their auras to create an unbroken circle while the opening prayer is said. This will create a ring of linked auras. The prayer to the Creator will give thanks for the love, learning and guidance of the Divine Light during the meeting. Thanks will also be given for the guides, Angels and helpers who'll be present. The prayer will ask for protection from all the negativity in the world.

## White Light Meditation

If the 'Blue Sky Preparation' has done its job, your mind could be clearer and open to spiritual thoughts. The White Light Mediation can take you to another level of calm:

- Breath rhythmically, feet flat on the floor, back pressed comfortably against the chair, palms of your hands lying flat on your thighs. Close your eyes.

- Imagine a solid cone of sparkling white light hovering above the crown of your head.

- Switch you attention to the soles of your feet. Draw up the magnetic energy from Mother Earth. Feel the strong heavy vibration slowly slide up to your ankles and calves to your knees in rolling waves.

- Switch focus back to your head, as the brilliant, white light lowers to the top of your head and suffuse downwards. You may feel the crackling static of electricity mess with your hair. The raw energy slides downwards, through your neck and over your shoulders.

- The healing warmth relaxes and soothes. The two energies meet and swirl as one in your solar plexus. Your entire body is encased in pure, white light.

- Feel that sensation. Open your eyes. Get ready to raise your chakra energies and connect with spirit.

## Raising Your Energies and Awakening the Spiritual You

Awakening the spiritual 'you' is to appreciate and understand the power of positive energies around you. Here's a practical way of raising the colours and positions of the chakra energies. It begins with mentally opening the red base chakra and then concentrating on each of the others in turn:

1. Sit on a chair with feet flat on the floor. Take off your shoes. Be warm and comfortable; play some soothing music in the background if you wish. Choose a time when you're the less likely to be disturbed.

2. Visualise the 7 stages of the chakras like a column of traffic lights positioned one above the other about 12"/30 cms in front of you. The colour order begins with red, then orange, yellow, green, blue, purple and white light.

3. Red: In your mind, switch on each light, one at a time. Turn on the red light, the first traffic light, positioned low in the pelvic area, called the base position. Cover yourself in red light from head to foot.

4. Orange: hold that feeling for a moment then switch in the orange traffic light. (This could be the sumptuous orange/bronze of a Buddhist monk's robe) at the Sacral level. Orange is at the solar plexus level, a very physical point where you instinctively feel 'gut reaction.'

5. Yellow: is the colour is at the spleen level, just under the rib cage, that helps us sense good and bad emotions.

6. Green: then switch to green of the heart centre that helps us deal with events impacting upon us. The heart chakra is the link point between physical centres and centres for higher spiritual communication. It is the heart chakra that Mediums use in combination with the throat, third eye centre and top crown chakra when connecting with Spirit.

7. Blue: for the throat. The throat is for inspirational speaking and when spirit uses a Medium's vocal cords.

8. Purple: is the 3$^{rd}$ Eye position for communication with Spirit.

9. White: at the top of your head or crown is your link with God, your guides and also links with your source of spiritual energy, providing the sustenance that your spirit needs.

As these lights shine inside your head, the pulsed energy heightens. The concentration deepens and strengthens. In a spiritual circle, with a number of people lending their thought energies to the process, the tempo increases. They add to the pace by bringing the energy up through one chakra to the next by thinking (in our example 'turn on the first red light') 'open centre one, open quicken and expand', then, 'open centre two, open quicken and expand'. This repetition drives the power of thought ever higher, right up to the seventh chakra point at the top of your head.

The 2$^{nd}$ Orange, 3$^{rd}$ Yellow and 4$^{th}$ Green positions are used in Healing, Auric Reading, Psychometry and Psychic Mediumship. Auric Reading is the studying and interpretation of your aura. Mediums can 'read' the colour of your aura to indicate your mental or physical health and colour can be a personality and character guide as well. Psychometry is frequently used in circle training sessions as a psychic exercise as you're about to see.

## The Training Session

Members of the circle will raise their energies inside their minds as the host Medium takes them through different chakra patterns and combinations, as mentioned in the previous paragraph. Chakra six, at the $3^{rd}$ Eye position in the centre of the brow is the communication centre with your guide. The energy builds as the intensity increases. The Medium will then ask everyone to connect with their guide. After a few moments of quiet, the host will ask members how they felt, what sensations they experienced and if they communicated with their guide. Connecting with your guide is a gradual blending. It takes dedication, practice and hard work. It can take some time for this to happen and needs the right motivation. Everyone has their own natural level of psychic ability. Not everyone is destined to become clairvoyant but everyone can follow their own path of advancement in healing or psychic intuition.

## Psychometry Practice

The host Medium will provide encouragement and give coaching advice to members of the group. Members are paired together and, sitting opposite each other, see if they can 'get anything' for each other. Their psychic skills are stimulated by playing card games, shuffling a pack with different symbolic images. The players choose two cards each at random, and interpret the meanings for their partner. This exercise draws on psychometry and involves creating a mental image of a person and their personality. A bed of soft sand lies upon a tray. The tray is placed out of sight of the members. The members close their eyes. One person at a time moves away from the group and presses a palm into the sand without the others seeing them. They return to their seat. The others open their eyes and a volunteer goes to the tray. Their hand hovers over the palm depression in the sand. They have to 'sense' whose hand print it is and describe them. The same kind of exercise can be done with people leaving a personal item, for example a broach, a set of keys, or an earring. Members try to match the item with the owner.

## Closing the Circle

When the training session ends, chairs are once again placed in a circle. Having opened their chakras and minds to Spirit, it is time to close down. The host Medium leads. Each chakra is mentally closed from white to red, from head to hips. The host may ask everyone to imagine they have a cape or sleeping bag covering them and protecting them from negative energies. A final prayer of thanks is said and Spirit closes the meeting with the word Amen. It is good to realise that we can open and close ourselves to spirit. Spirit doesn't have 'control' over us all the time. It is a two-way relationship. Also, on the same theme, when we speak about negative energies we mean the power that negative actions and feelings create in this world. You know the force that anger has you can sense anger physically pushing against you. This energy disperses and rises into the atmosphere and hangs there. It is this negativity that we guard against.

## Coming Next:

Until now we have given an introduction to spirituality, described the work of Mediums and shown how we can connect with our guides. To many people, witnessing clairvoyance in action and receiving messages from the other side of life is their first encounter and first evidence of life after physical death. That is the start of a series of revelations. This chapter will describe the perpetual partnership between our world and the world of Spirit; a dynamic partnership that affects every aspect of our lives positively. We work together. We are Spirit. Spirit are us.

# CHAPTER FIVE

# Our Partnership with Spirit

Our partnership with Spirit is a living thing. The spirit world is all around us. It is in the ether. It is invisible to the human eye but not the human mind. We sense, we feel, the presence of Spirit through our intuition. We communicate through the channel of thought energy. It is a relationship of equals. Equals who shared this world together living on earth as physical beings but now share it in mind and thought.

This chapter will provide examples of the humanity of Spirit. It will be brought to you in messages of love and understanding. It will provide examples of how Spirit is constantly looking out for us.

## Talking to each other

Before we begin, here's a recap on how the interaction works. Janet makes contact with her guides and they pass messages using mind-to-mind transfer. Spirits are the transmitters. Janet translates the messages and gives them to me to place in the book. As I am the final destination, spirits address the messages to me as the writer. That's why my name is featured in the examples you're about to read, I'm the final post box.

## The Scribe

The Scribe describes how we work together as our two worlds communicate:

"People of your world have misconceptions of how Spirit work with the human mind. Most think it is for clairvoyance, healing, artistry and the communication of Spirit to the person on the earth who wishes to hear from a loved one. We are thought combined with energy and we can use these thoughts in any way we wish. In your case, it is through your own thought waves that we are channeling, to give you the confidence, the correct words to use in certain situations. This does not necessarily mean it is only for the use, and guidance of your spiritual work, you are being helped in your material life. The failings many have on your earth is to forget that Spirit bring forth many other attributes such as courage, wisdom, faith, patience, trust, clarity, obedience, discipline. We are there to help, teach, guide and encourage you through all of life's trials."

## Running Water

Frequently, we work with groups of guides as well as speaking to individuals. This piece describes the working relationship with the group headed by Running Water in this letter to me in my role as the writer:

"My dear, respected friend,

How pleasing it has become to us, as a group, that we can make contact with you, how and when we wish, through either the written word or verbal conversations.

The importance of being able to have the contact is vital for you and also for our development as a group. Yes, my friend, we are all developing together to secure the binding of our relationships. You would agree that when an agreement has been made between two parties to work together as one, especially when one of the parties has to be reliant on the other; it then becomes a situation where trust plays the most important part. We lead to pave the way ahead for you so, therefore, my friend, you have to trust us. You then become reliant upon us that we are leading you in the right direction. This, my friend, is unquestionable as we have become aware that you will follow us, without any questions in your own mind of hesitation or uncertainty as to whether it is the right path for you to follow. You have learnt to trust.

It is a most enjoyable experience to be able to speak to you verbally. We can broach many subjects or just have a conversation between friends. My role in this vast network of working energies; is most important and, that is, I have been awarded the role of being the one energy that guards and protects our special light of communication. We can use Janet as a channeler for conversations which is a joy for any spirit to be able to work with and we also channel through her mind to write our letters.

I will explain why we have decided to use the two roads of communication. You may wonder 'why don't the spirits just speak verbally through her, surely it would save time?' Verbal conversations are not only so we can blend in with her energies; they also give us the link into your energies while you are relaxed and concentrating on the meeting in hand. You are skillfully playing an important part in allowing us to blend our energies into your own energy field, without you becoming aware of what is actually happening.

It can take many years for people to reach that fine blend of energies that are needed for the work you have agreed to follow. We have given you a short cut. This can only happen with the commitment and dedication of that you have shown. You will now only ever move forward and not backwards. Also, by the verbal communications, we can get to know each other. You have the hard job of identifying certain spirits by the way they speak, by the energies that surround you and also by the tone of the voice. You have fallen into step with this role easily and the confidence is growing with each meeting that is taking place.

We can laugh together, speak personally and directly about anything that is troubling you and give you peace of mind, and also answer any questions that you may have. The only downside of this way of communication is that, through conversations, one question or subject can easily lead onto many different roads or outlets, therefore cutting down on the main topic of importance. Vital pieces of information can at times be left unsaid. As you have become very aware, when any of the spirits choose to speak, they can be very reluctant to leave therefore using up much of the valuable time that is allowed us. There are many energies that have the power to be able to communicate verbally through Janet and, at times, it can be difficult for all the information to be given; plus, the energies can cause interference to the spirit who is conversing at the given time.

There is also another way in which we work and that, my friend, is our intuition, or, as we often say it is our gut instinct. This we know is becoming very obvious and common to you now. You have adjusted very quickly to our way of working and thinking. The best time for us to work in this way is during your sleep state, that is when you are at your most relaxed and it is easier for our energies to blend in with yours. If a thought is continuously there, outlined in your thought waves, then you know that we have been to work. It is likened to a switch being turned on.

My friend, I hope that this has been of some help to you and has been explained with the simplicity that we like to carry through with our work. We felt that an explanation was due to you on this subject.

My energies will now fade until another time. Your most trusted friend Running Water."

Understanding Spirit would not be the same without learning about them as human beings. They were, and are, just like us. These are a few personal stories. It's like having a heart-to-heart with a close friend from across the universe.

## Josiah

Josiah was a Quaker. He lived in Virginia, USA about 150 years ago at the time of the American Civil War. Josiah is a poet and a hopeless romantic. These are his words:

"Here is a little glimpse into my life:

We would have lived in a very close-knit community and my upbringing was one of love and affection. It would have been a daily or nightly vigil of reading verses or chapters from the Bible or as some would like to name it the 'good book'. We would not have preached to others; if they wished to join us then very welcomed they would be. Our purpose in life was to be peace loving people who would respect and help those who could not help themselves. If you feed the soul with love it can become like a beacon that shines throughout all kinds of misery.

My betrothal to Eliza was always meant to be. To my eyes, she was a wonder to bestow with her skin the colour of cream and the hair of golden wheat. We were born to be sweethearts and friends forever. She replaced the good nature of my mother and became my soul mate. We were blessed with four children. One who was taken straight from birth and another one taken in infancy through the fever. The other two grew to be strong and lived well past our ages. Although we grieved those who were lost to us, we understood that, at times, sacrifices are made so that we left on earth can understand the hardships of others less fortunate than ourselves. We would go to their graves and bless the earth where they stayed and recite: 'My dear little ones, you were sent from Heaven to earth for a short time to bring your blessings from above. Like most Angels your time was short because you had more important work to do in Heaven. Shine my darling souls; you will be in our hearts forever until our return.'

Eliza and I would sit out on the verandah in the evening under the night sky conversing on many a subject. Through her calming voice and the relaxation of the sweet smell of the night air, I would go to my desk and the words would start to once again flow from my thoughts, down the arm into the hand, along the stem of the quill and spill out onto the parchment; and there I would stay until the dawning of the day. It would be at times such as this where the inspiration would flow.

Life, my friend, is a precious gift, as precious as the earth you walk upon. Cherish yourself and cherish the earth. It is the earth who feeds and nourishes, not only the body but also the soul. The beauty and wonders all around you are indeed a gift from the great Creator. We are on loan to the earth for but a short while and it's the duty of all to protect all you see.

You see now, my friend, how relaxed I am in your company that it comes naturally to be able to share my thoughts from my inner being. Are we not very similar in nature where we would rather love than fight? The love of the words tumbling around in the mind brings upon us a tingling of excitement to be able to share with others.

My friend, it is time now for my energies to fade until another time.

Your friend forever, Josiah"

Josiah shares his love of family in this very personal letter to me. It shows the strength of our friendship and respect for one another and agreement of 'family first'.

"My dear friend,

Would you agree with me when I say that families are a very important part of our lives? They can create within us that unconditional love that is only reserved for those special people who walk into our lives at any given time.

Needless to say, our kin who we have created or who have created us are a fixture within our hearts regardless of any hurt or upsets they may cause. Our parents are there to love and guide us through all the difficulties of adjusting back into living in a physical body. The baby is born and comes with all the love from spirit and is placed within the loving arms of its mother. From then on the journey begins, not only for the child but also for whoever is responsible for guiding that child on their pathway. It is a difficult task to be responsible for someone so young and innocent, with all the harshness and cruelties that life can bring.

For the parent or guardian, the seed of love is sown from the birth of the infant and, over time, that seed grows and grows. It is like a tree growing from a small seedling and over times gains strength. It can be kicked at, chopped at, beaten with sticks or metal objects. The branches can be pulled or cut but the tree will never waver because it is solid in strength and will always continue to be there if ever needed. Indeed Stephen, the tree with all its branches can shield from any storms. With its strong trunk it can be leaned on in times of woe or just for comfort. With its healing properties, it can give that inner strength and food for the soul. It can also listen and never pass judgement. It has the same qualities as being a parent or guardian.

My mother was my solid tree. She was always there guiding me and protecting me away from all the harshness of the world. It was her who led me onto the path of which I choose to follow and, until the end of my days she instilled within me the love and respect for others. My father died in my infancy, leaving just myself and my mother and, from then on in, she became my sole protector and keeper.

When the time came for me to change pathways, from her to Eliza, it came with her full support and love. It was then our turn to shield and protect her.

When my son and daughter started to grow and be shaped by their personalities (it is here Stephen that I have discovered another similarity between us two, for you also have a son and daughter). My first thoughts were 'Josiah you have to shed any inadequacy of how you feel about becoming the master of your home and let your children see within you the inner strength which is needed when you are up against people with strong minds and opinions'. Because, Stephen, that is what they are; people. They may have been born from your seed but they are only on loan to us until they find their own strength to follow their own individual pathway.

Your children have been raised with unconditional love which has placed them in a position of self-respect and independence. Your daughter has a soul which is surrounded by the love and light of the Creator and she will only gain more strength as she continues to grow and develop. She spreads light and contentment wherever she goes. There is also a similarity there Stephen between her and my Ruth.

Your son still needs the nearness of the tree although he likes his independence. There is still that stray tendril attached which gives him a feeling of security and togetherness. He will find his own way in time. He thinks deep and suffers in silence. To others he is a free spirit; to himself he is a closed book. Have no worries Stephen where your children are concerned; the light of the Creator is shining above both their heads. The decisions they will have to make will be with love and guidance.

There is that 'other' family; those who are connected by near or distant blood or those who have found their way into our hearts. Some stay and some go. Each time you lose someone's love, it is like a small part of the heart has died, but with time, the heart can heal and learn to love again. Love is there with you and for you Stephen. Don't reject it. All love is sent to you from the Creator it can come in many different ways and means. It can be a smile from your mother, it can be the butterfly fluttering around your person, it can be a wave or a handshake from a stranger or it can come in the form of another being, whose only desire is to share love and be loved without any obligations. It is there for everyone and it is there for you. The Lord looks out for all his flock and what better reward can he give than love.

You see now, Stephen, how completely at ease and confident I am in your company. My letter writing is giving me back my own identity. My spirit is awakened and once again very active.

Your friend Josiah, with love from the heart."

Josiah wrote this poem by candlelight. He sent it to Janet to pass on to you.

The Angel of the Night
The colour of the sky is ink black
Yet the air is crystal clear
There is a shadow across the moon
Did you see it move? Where did it go?
It is unseen against the blackness of the sky
Yet you can see the wings flutter in the darkness
You can feel the love float in from the breeze.
There it is again, up against the light of the moon
Aah! It is the Angel of the Night keeping watch
It looks, it sees, it blinks its eyes
It flutters it wings then the stars shine like twinkling lights
And shower the world with love and protection
You are never alone when the Angel of the night is there
She is the Mother of all for your protection.
When the dawn breaks she rests her wings until dusk
Then her nightly vigil will once again take place.
Keep safe my children of the earth,
Your lives are precious gifts,
You were sent from us to live a life
Cherish your days on the earth
Love your brothers and sisters
You are all God's children

Shake your neighbour's hand with a smile upon your face
Forgo wars and hatred, instead unite and love each other
You all live as one under God's sky
Breathe in the warmth and the love which He sends to you
For you are all the children of God.
My energies will now retire. Your forever friend Josiah."

## Sister Theresa

Sister Theresa opens our minds to the work of the caring professions on the other side of life. Interestingly, doctors, nurses and carers tend to continue their vocation when they pass. Sister Theresa, who likes to be known as Christina, lived in the Middle Ages and caught a fever from the patients she was tending.

"My dear Stephen, you can't imagine the sheer joy it was when Running Water said 'Christina, you have been given permission to write a note to Stephen.' Straight away my thoughts were overcome with excitement, then I thought, Christina calm down, because you have been given this one chance so use it wisely.

As you are aware, my energies are following within the realms of the caring profession. This means that we care for many of the souls who return to Spirit who need to be cared for, due to certain traumas they may have experienced either in passing or in certain circumstances leading up to the end of their earthly existence. This is a rewarding task for us to be able to undertake. Some of these souls have led extremely difficult lives. Many of them would have suffered greatly at the mercy of others, either through physical violence or mental cruelty. Others would have led a very lonely and difficult life feeling excluded from the rest of humanity, causing them to distance themselves from others and thus feel completely alone in your world.

Many of these souls would try to make sense of their earthly lives by grasping onto every breath they take, but at the same time, longing for the peace and security of the Homeland. When they are eventually returned to us they are sent to our energies to heal their souls, before they start their onwards journey back to within the realms.

To live a life upon your earth doesn't always mean it is a life of happiness and joy; for some it can be a terrible burden. There is that silent thought within every soul that gives them the desire and determination to cling onto life for all its worth despite the fact that inside they are mourning for the return to the Homeland. It is these spirits that we care for and heal back to their own abilities to feel safe and secure once again. Once our work is done then they are released back into the atmosphere to start upon their journey.

The people of your earth can at times be cruel to each other with the thoughtless words and sentences they use to shield themselves from harm. They forget to think and care for others because they can only think and care for themselves. This is also where we can be of some help. When a person of your earth is suffering from someone's cruelty, whether it is physically or mentally, we have mass healing ceremonies to transfer the healing powers from our world to help those who suffer.

That is just a small part of my work here in Spirit. It has given me much delight in being able to write my thoughts onto paper, for you to be able to read at any time you wish.

Sister Theresa - but I like you to know me as Christina."

## Jimmy

We met Jimmy in Chapter Three. He introduced himself as a soldier who fought in the First World War. Every year in the UK we hold a Remembrance Day Parade to honour all those combatants in past conflicts and for those who are fighting and dying in today's wars. Jimmy wrote this beautiful poem as someone who'd experienced the horror of trench warfare. It is also a touching example of how Spirit is so in-tune with our world and understands the pain and anguish we feel. The poem was received a day before the 2019 ceremony. On the 11$^{th}$ day of the 11$^{th}$ month we posted it online and read it out loud to church congregations in commemoration. Although it was written for that year, his words, the message, will stand the test of time:

## Remembrance Day 11th November

A Poem by Jimmy

'We marched in step side by side all in a line
Come join us, all will be fine,
Off to war we went to fight for King and Country
All young boys were we, short and tall, fat and thin
But what a mess we've found ourselves in
Boots shiny, jackets and trousers all new
Hair cut, short back and sides
Off we went to fight for our lives
Across the water we sailed
After we waved goodbye to our pals

Family and friends lined up to shout
'Good luck and show them what it's all about'
We landed on ground all fired up and ready to go
With hope in our hearts and fight in our soul
It won't take long they said
You will be back home in months, all ready for bed

One year followed another
The tears flowed free; will we ever be set free?
Telegrams came and went as the coffins stacked up
The injured went home all broken inside
Will this nonsense ever subside?
The bullets fly from one side to the other
Each killing one another, brother to brother

Don't cry for us, be proud instead
That we laid down our lives with pride and not dread
It's a duty we all shared
So you could all walk forward in life and be spared
We still march on, shoulder to shoulder
Each and every one of us with our spirit growing bolder
We shine our light to you in your land
When it's your time we will take you by the hand

We stepped onto the ladder of light
With our souls once again shining bright
Fears all left behind and peace in our hearts
Do not grieve for us because we all played our part.
War goes on, will man never learn?
To kill each other is a sin
Open you hearts and let the peace live within.

Jimmy

Often, Spirit like to converse, and send their thoughts to us, not to teach but to connect. Grey Dove wanted to share this on Love and Peace. It was prompted by a close friend who had suffered a tragic loss. It was a chance for Grey Dove to speak of the healing power of love and demonstrate that Spirit is ever watchful, caring and sending us love.

## Love and Peace

"On your earth, as a living being, you have an emotional toolbox of energy to draw upon. Some people keep emotions buried; they do not use them at all. For your soul to be complete, you need to experience every emotion in your psyche. Your whole spiritual pod of energy must learn. Some people bury emotion as it gives much anguish and rejection, and can cause excruciating pain. Love, there is love within everyone; love, light, peace, wrapped up in a parcel of spiritual protection. You come back to earth to live and learn from one another, to learn right from wrong, to sift love and hate. The bright, white light of the Creator is there. It flickers within every one of us. By believing in yourself, you believe in the particle of energy from God that is within you.

Peace will never be everywhere on earth. There's always someone, somewhere who wants to disturb that peace. Think hard; if everyone was kind to one another, if peace abounds, no one would learn anything. It is through the challenges and our reaction to those tests that we learn and develop. The lessons you learn are invaluable. Love conquers all. The most common question for our world is 'why'? Why does God let that happen? God gives you life but does not tell you how to run your life. Why do some go against everything that's good? Some like to gather that great big ball of power. Good always conquers evil. You don't come back to live a life of misery. It's a harsh world living in a physical incarnation, but the lessons you learn are invaluable. People who start the bad things in life are lost and smothered. Love is beyond any measure you could ask for. It is the most powerful emotional tool you possess.

A mother has lost her only daughter; taken from her by a most heinous crime. What words can Spirit say to put the trust back for that person? We can say that the daughter is now happy in the spiritual realms. Gradually, step by step, the parents have to mend themselves but at times don't know how to do this. So they go within themselves. A bitter pill starts to form. They've taken it personally. A callous wedge has been placed between them. They are experiencing grief in the highest form. We cover them with the light of the Creator for protection from grief and negativity. The father is trying to forget what happened to ease his pain. The mother wonders if she is to blame in some way, could she, should she, have taken her beautiful daughter out of harm's way? We try to lighten the load. A black cloud consumes them. We cannot lift the veil of grief, for it is an emotion that is in every one of you. But we can place our energies on these people. They will have to find their own way. We can help people get through the dense darkness within them. They ask 'why did God let this happen?' God never lets anything happen, that's Man. That's what mankind does. They fight against one another. They behave in ways that are unacceptable. But love is there, it flickers the whole time and it never gets diminished.

I leave you with my parting words. Never let that love die within you. Let that love reach out to everyone that you touch. Love comes in all different shapes and forms. You can love people in many different ways. If that love shines out from within then you are a happier person within. I leave you with the purity of love."

Grey Dove

## Coming Next:

In the next chapter we'll describe the concept of incarnation and re-incarnation, of past and future lifetimes rolling forward. Spirit is your everlasting state of being. With each earthly lifetime, you will gain knowledge and progress until at last you are as one with the divine. Living and learning continue. The concept of incarnation is the engine that drives the eternal cycle. It helps us appreciate the notion of eternal time filled with repeated incarnations.

# CHAPTER SIX

# The Eternal You

"Before you were born you were pure energy in the world of Spirit. This purity of Spirit is with you at birth in the material world. Simultaneaously your soul, the beating heart of your human emotions, joins your life from that moment onwards. Spirit and soul become one. When your time on earth is over you return to Spirit shaped by the life you have led." Blue Flame, Native American Indian.

When created by the Divine Spirit you were a single, individual atom of thought energy. That is your original, infinite and everlasting spiritual identity.

You are God's creation. You were created as an individual entity of spiritual energy. A sphere of pure, white light, a pod of pure thought energy. As energy you are indestructible. Your spirit is immortal. It evolves as a unique spirit in human form from birth to passing. When this earthly lifetime comes to a close, your spirit ascends from your physical body to return to the realms of Spirit.

Your original incarnation became your first life in physical form. This lifetime is your latest and current re-incarnation. You can describe it as a re-birth of your spirit. Every incarnation is a learning and developmental experience. Each is your spiritual self being born again to experience a new life. You will encounter emotional, mental and physical challenges. You will face obstacles to overcome. Free-will and intuition, your conscience and sense of right and wrong will be your guide.

Being human, you're bound to make mistakes and probably cause pain and anguish. But, being human, you can make amends, atone for your actions, ask forgiveness and achieve love and happiness beyond measure. It is how you show love and kindness, how you look after others and how you value and protect this planet that charts a way forward.

Through the process of incarnation, you will experience all the different versions of yourself. You will live through the many different aspects of your character and personality. You will experience the full spectrum of emotions as Grey Dove explained. It is as if you have an emotional toolbox holding every element of every emotion. The good, the fine, the noble are side by side with the mean, the nasty, the cruel and the spiteful. They are all inside the toolbox. Eventually your Book of Life will be complete. You and you alone will be the judge of how you did, you are not judged by others. If there is more work needing to be done, another lifetime will beckon.

In the fullness of time, you will once again achieve purity of spirit. This is when the spiritual cycle will have turned full circle, from a pure pod of thought energy back to pure white energy.

This is how Wang Chang explained how our emotions are the instruments of change:

"You have many lifetimes. The emotional toolbox you possess affects the way you feel. In one lifetime people may concentrate on the emotions of jealousy and negativity. They go through their life with these emotions dominating. All the other emotions would be secondary. Once you have used certain emotions to the full, there is no need to experience those emotions to the same extent again. You then draw upon other emotions in other lifetimes until you exhaust them all. One person may come back and draw on the emotions of happiness and love for a lifetime and not draw on others. Some people may have one, two or three incarnations. Some people have more than that. The majority of people use up to six or seven incarnations, as it takes a long time to experience all the emotions in the emotional toolbox. The experience you have gained will continue to grow in Spirit while you are living another lifetime."

While certain emotions are given priority, it does not mean the others are not experienced at all. It is a subtle blending for the spirit to realise the impact each emotion can create. Some emotions in the toolbox are used frequently, others rarely. Happiness is joyful and uplifting. Negative energies are the reverse. With each incarnation the returning spirit will gain a greater insight into human nature. The resulting knowledge depends upon the nature, personality and spiritual character of the individual. And, of course, the type of incarnation they have experienced. The impact of nature and nurture will play a pivotal role. If a spirit has lived an opulent lifestyle in one incarnation but another in poverty the pressures of life will have totally changed and so will the learning experience. When all the emotions are experienced and implications understood, then the spirit can continue to ascend within the realms of spirit on their return. The Sunflower of God can help explain.

## The Sunflower of God

Here's a thought. Visualise a single, beautiful sunflower. The sunflower represents an individual spirit. The sunflower is you. The roots and stem support the flower head surrounded by lush green leaves. The flower head holds the sunflower seeds. Think of each seed as a separate spiritual incarnation. Every incarnation experiences different emotions, in different ways, in different genders, at different times in different places, within different social circles. One by one, the seeds live their lifetimes and return to the mother flower. When every seed has returned, the journey is complete. The flower is made whole once again. The spirit is made whole once again, as we will be.

## Learning and Unlearning

Every incarnation is a different learning experience. In the 'sunflower' example, a returning seed will bring back knowledge from emotions at a particular time. When a different seed begins a fresh incarnation it begins with a separate set of emotional goals. Importantly, this clean sheet is exactly that - clean. There is no memory of any previous incarnation to affect the new one. This is so a spirit can live a new life, making their free-will decisions, without being influenced by past behaviour. Past incarnations are 'unlearned' until the spirit has completed the emotional cycle. The Spirit Elders will decide which emotional journey of discovery and advancement you'll experience with each rebirth.

This is how Shining Star put it:

"When deciding to once again return to the earth, the returning spirit will gain a further insight into human nature and its many complexities. You need to cherish and learn from the life you are leading at the time. When the spirit has decided to return it's as if it is that spirit's very first time and all memories from previous existences are erased. This allows each life to be a fresh experience unfettered by past influences. Each new life and everything learned during that lifetime continues to shape the soul and will contribute to a spirit's evolution.

When that new life is over, the experience gained will feed back into the main energy from whence it came, in other words, into the primal soul of the individual spirit. You can liken it to a parted pod of life experience rejoining others, until it is whole again, and satisfied with what has been learnt along the way. Knowledge and understanding increases until it can go no further. What is waiting is the Divine Light then your spirit evaporates into the purity of the light, the purity of the Creator.

It's only in your world where colour and creed matter. Geographical location, wealth or poverty is all for your world. The spirit would have chosen what they can add to the wealth of knowledge that they have gained or avoided. This will include how they can enhance the knowledge they will bring back to our world. Would they choose to suffer, would they choose to do wrong? No, my friend. They are the experiences that happen once the spirit is living in a physical form. The choices they have made or have been made for them start to shape their lives.

How else can each returning spirit learn if they are not prepared to experience everything that life can throw at them?"

## A little more learning

Running Water wanted to give more detail on how an incarnation can affect the soul:

"Every incarnation is a two-way journey for both a physical and a spiritual being. They start the journey together at the same time as a beating heart and a spiritual soul. Take the soul away and the heart still beats but you have an empty vessel. Put the soul back in and a life form takes place.

The physical form may not be in perfect health. The person may be blind or deaf. They may have mental problems. They could be disfigured. They could suffer from any number of ailments during the incarnation. The soul would know that they are about to embark on a journey where they would learn many things. But they would not know the state of the body they would live in. They may experience being bullied or become the subject of ridicule, or being physically or mentally abused. The soul would learn throughout their humanity all these different challenges and how to cope with them.

This incarnation would be to teach the soul to be more understanding when they come back home to Spirit. That could be the lesson of that rebirth."

## Gender is an earth issue

At conception, your spirit joins your physcial body for this current incarnation. Previous incarnations could be in a either a male or female gender. Your spirit does not have a gender. Only when you adopt a physical body does gender come into the equation, as determined by your parents.

When you pass back into Spirit and revert to your spiritual identity, your mind and thought intelligence recalls and responds to any communication with the earth plane in the correct gender manner. A Medium would describe the appearance and personality of the person in a way that people here on earth would recognise. Your friends and family would identify with the person they loved.

## Good & Bad

You are already living through a wide range of emotions during this incarnation. Following what Wang Chang said, are you aware that certain emotions dominate? Or you can look at yourself and sense a pattern? You too could realise that you are going through a particular learning period where certain emotions are in evidence. Becoming aware of them could be a window in your mind to change your behavior or to somehow look at yourself from outside your body, to notice the action/reaction process that is happening, and do something about it. It could be a kind of dynamic self- assessment where you alter your thinking or attitude while life is happening around you.

In our daily lives, we all have good and bad days. Generally nothing's too extreme. We upset others and get upset. We get bad moods and act selfishly. We hurt and get hurt. We can feel guilty and make amends. We can feel aggrieved and want to retaliate. This is the normal way of things. We can apologise, forgive or ask forgiveness and move on.

You may wonder what happens to a person who has committed serious crimes or has inflicted pain on others, someone you'd describe as being bad or evil? What happens when these people pass into spirit? There are no manacles or torture. No purgatory or a burning pit of Hell. Instead they face an extreme period of atonement. They are still Spirit and the Creator will not deny them a prolonged path to eventual redemption. They will enter a realm of dense energy, a kind of spiritual solitary confinement, where they would ask forgiveness for everything they've done and every person they've hurt. This would take time outside our understanding. This would be until they eventually progress toward the Divine Light. When they're in this dense energy, they will not be able to make contact with anyone on earth. Spirit cannot reward anyone who has gone against the laws of the spiritual realms. By the same token the Divine Light will never be denied to a soul seeking redemption.

## Coming Next:

This next chapter is about the passage through life in broad terms. Every journey has its own special spiritual purpose. Every journey has its time. Your purpose is to live life with all its twists and turns, with all its joys and challenges, with all its love and learning.

## CHAPTER SEVEN

# The Earthly Cycle of Life

Books talk about the seven ages of man, from birth to ripe, old age. That may be the perfect mortal cycle but life isn't like that. Life is on-loan and might be recalled at any point. Chapter Seven will look at the cycle from a spiritual angle. We will talk about aspects that you'll encounter and provide some food for thought on how to cope with the challenges. After all, life on earth is a learning and developmental cycle, a kind of physical and emotional assault course.

We'll begin *before* the beginning. Before your parents met and way before Cupid's arrow found its mark, your spirit was preparing for a rebirth. You would not know where you would live, or whether you would be born into riches or poverty or what kind of parents you would have. Would they adore you? Would you be wanted? Would you be healthy? Would you live a long life? These decisions would have been made depending on what your spirit needed to learn and experience during this incarnation. The one you're enjoying now. Those big decisions would depend on how many past lives you had led and where you were in your progression through the Realms of Spirit. But, for now, let's switch back to life on earth.

## The Ticking Clock of Mortality

We live our lives by the ticking clock of mortality. Using time well is a popular theme of Spirit, as time is on loan and we never know when the lifelong debt will be called in.

This is Brown Bear's message:

"My dear, trusted friend,

Time waits for no man; isn't that an expression which is used widely upon your earth?

The importance of time governs your whole lives. Everything is done to a schedule. There is never enough time. Have you run out of time, is it too late? Has time now expired, limiting you as to what you do, to what you want to achieve? The years have gone past at such a speed. Are you a slave to time? Many wasted years have gone before you and is it now too late for you to enjoy many of the experiences that are there to achieve and enjoy?

If only I had the presence of mind to use the power of thought to make good use of the time that was given to me. Many valuable minutes have been wasted because of the lack of knowledge within me to understand that life is a precious gift to enjoy to and make the most of those minutes.

It is only as we grow and develop that we learn many of life's lessons. At times our minds are too busy with the past to make the most of the present and the future.

At youth, a person will think many years ahead and will automatically come to the conclusion that time is plentiful. There is no need to rush, time is on my side, that is what the future is for. I can achieve many of my wishes and desires in good time and be able to learn new experiences to be passed onto others. There is enough time for me to learn.

They then find themselves caught up in living, caught up within many of the disturbances that can surround you, holding you back and keeping you from moving forward, then suddenly time has elapsed and gone. With it, is many of the hopes and dreams that you wanted to achieve and all those ideas of learning something new to experience and enjoy were only dreams. The chance to rekindle those thoughts are washed away forever because, through time, you have lost your youth, and along with it, the opportunity has gone.

A spirit will return to earth to live a life in a physical body. From the moment of birth the clock of life will gradually start to tick away; the seconds go into minutes, the minutes will go into hours, then to days, then to months, to years. The tick of the clock will silently move on during the lifetime of that person, never knowing when it's to stop. For some, it is like waiting for an explosion, to be extinguished back into Eternity: never knowing what to expect, never knowing what is waiting for them on the other side. For others, it is like waiting for that eternal rest and peace which will shadow their energy and leave them in an eternal existence of pure love.

There is one certainty that comes with the new life. That is that time is on loan.

The length of the loan is a guarded secret. It's for people to make the most of while they are on your earth. How much knowledge and experience and life's lessons will they manage to achieve during their lifetime? Life is not a rehearsal. Everything that is done cannot be undone. Mistakes are made and hopefully learned by; life's lessons can be shared with others so that we can enrich them with the knowledge we have gained during our years, and thus make good use of our time on the earth.

To make the most of your life is not to put off until the morrow what you can do today. Follow your thoughts and plans. Learn new things. Make the most of every day that comes, enjoy as much as you can and even when things go wrong, always try to look at the positive side. Disappointments come and go. They should never hold you back, only spur you on towards your goal. Make the most of every day. You cannot bring it back once it's gone.

Life is precious. You can liken it to a piece of clay, if you shape it with care and thought, you will take pride in what you have achieved but if you leave it to itself, then regrets will form when you see the lacklustre results."

Your friend, Brown Bear

Months have passed since that note from Brown Bear. Josiah had been quiet in his writings before his take on time was received by Janet two nights ago, when we were in the midst of the Coronavirus outbreak:

"The interaction between a spiritual energy and a Spirit in the physical is one that, for me, is very special. The connection is one of a harmonisation that can only be achieved by pure thought.

You may have wondered why there has been an absence in the writings from Josiah. The answer is time. It's the nothingness of time in our world and yet in your world it's the important part of your life that can never be changed, altered or stopped. It is continuous. It flows from minute to minute just like the flowing of the river, never ending and never stopping. Time is like a journey rolling on and on into pastures new. You can never catch it. It is there in front of you moving every second, every time you try to catch a second it has gone.

Time for me is a second for every hour, day or month. It's irrelevant. We stretch out to reach the balance between your world and ours. We understand the importance of time to you on the earth; how certain things in your life can be affected by the lack of time, how certain things have to be put on hold because the time is not right.

When two minds are working together, one from Spirit and the other from your world, we have to create an ideal way of communication which involves the fluidity of time. The interaction between our energies have to keep in time with your fast moving lives.

At this moment in time, the people on your earth are experiencing uncertainty, changes, fear of the unknown and loss. You are all being tested to delve deep within your souls and inner being to deal with the situation that you all are experiencing. It can be likened to that of an unseen war which has been let loose upon your earth and you are all warriors working together to rid the earth of this silent attack.

Solidarity and the drawing of everyone's love and energy will help you all to unite together. Prayers for the living and prayers for those who return home are linked all around your world. It will end. In its wake, there will be many lessons learned, some to remember and some to forget. Through it, you will all remember time.

Time to give to your love ones, to your friends, to yourself. Time to do the many things that you have put on hold because you have been caught up in the furore of moving endlessly on without giving any thought to what you are doing. Just merely existing and not living. Time to create, time to take in the beauty of your earth, time to enjoy life. Time is precious. In years to come, people will always remember the time when the silent war invaded their lives and changes were made, and of how those changes altered the world.

# Tree of Life – Part Two: The Roots of Life

Earlier, we touched upon The Tree of Life as both a symbol of eternal life and a powerful aid to meditation. It doesn't end there. Blue Flame and The Scribe write about its significance to each of us, as a guide to living our material and spiritual lives. How clearly we define our purpose and goals and how we grow and progress is described using the roots, trunk and branches of the tree.

This is Blue Flame's approach:

"How well the tree is planted decides the material and spiritual pathway of a person's life-plan, from childhood to adulthood. One person's tree can be focused on the one thing they wish to reach for. Another cannot grasp what they are here to achieve. That person can't decide upon their direction and their roots are not strongly planted. One tree has an understanding of their spiritual direction, another could be all about their material wellbeing.

A young person starts to climb the Tree of Life. They encounter branches that represent different life choices. Which ones do they explore, where will it take them, will a branch be barren or full of fruit? Should I strive to get to the top of the tree and settle among the high branches? If I get to the top, will I fall and crash to the ground? Should I stay at a safe level and make the most of what I've gained? All these choices depend upon what success means to you. Do you want a pot of gold at the top of the tree? Or is your success what you bring to others; the difference you make to their lives?

You can always stop and climb back down onto another branch. Life is full of lessons that, once learned, can make you reconsider your options. It can be when, through time and experience, you look afresh and feel the guidance of spirit pulling at your soul. There's more to living than striving. Inevitably, every living soul will go back to spirit. Will it be with love or a sense of loss?"

Spirit consistently sends us love and guidance. The Scribe wanted to pass on his advice on living on earth and how to carve out a pathway to follow. He continues with his thoughts on the Tree of Life:

"The Tree of Life is deep-rooted. The tentacles of the branches entwine themselves around until they have to find another avenue or pathway to go. Each new pathway can be like a new mystery to walk along. There will be twigs and offshoots leading nowhere. This can cause irritations as to why you have wasted time in going along that way when you could have walked further on towards a goal of more fulfilment.

Every avenue has a purpose. Every breath that is taken and every minute of your day is precious. When you compare the time in your world to the time you are in Spirit then there is no comparison. You realise that every atom of time is to be cherished and learned by. Mistakes are vital to make, this is how you learn and progress. In my previous note, I spoke of the fool who will always try to cover his tracks, who will lay blame at the door of others. This person would have tried to climb their tree going straight up, not taking any twists or turns nor learning by mistakes that would have littered their path.

They would sneer at the wise man who would take the turnings that would present themselves. They would laugh in the face of those who would stand tall and admit to the mistakes they had made. They would learn nothing about human nature. Their main object would be to reach their goal at whatever costs it would be to others. They would have no goal set before them because, to them, the main objective of their life would be to live and not to learn. The wise man may always be a step behind. This is because they know that, when the fool falls, he needs a soft landing. The fool will never win. The wise man is not in a race to become the winner; he is there to learn from the life he has been given. He is there to care for others; the animals who walk your earth, the environment where he lives, the forests, the oceans and the planet. The wise person would live their Tree of Life to the full, exploring and learning every avenue until they have understood why they had been planted. Along the way, they may sigh at certain events that had taken place but each branch or twig they had walked would have made them into the person they would have become. By the time their Tree is ready to shed its leaves they would return a more contented spirit.

The fool would return with many regrets, not only for themselves but for others who they had brushed away with the flick of a hand, they would be longing to go back and climb their tree again to make adjustments and peace but it would be too late for that spirit once you have climbed your tree you do not get another chance in that incarnation.

My friend I am your humble servant. I bow before you with my parchments in my hands. I have been interrupted from my time in the Room of Scribes to converse with you in this manner which is a great pleasure and an honour for me to be able to do so."

## The Scribe

I wanted to lift these lines from the passage when the Scribe is talking about the wise man. Because it beautifully expresses why we are here and the human spirit by which we should lead our lives:

"He is there to care for others, the animals who walk your earth, the environment where he lives, the forests, the oceans and the planet. The wise person would live their tree of life to the full, exploring and learning every avenue until they have understood why they had been planted."

If we can follow these lines then our time on earth would be well spent. We will find out who we really are and be proud of ourselves in a way that is worthy of respect. Josiah continues the same emotion with these words:

"To love and bring peace upon the earth for everyone is God's desire. He will always be there to love and never judge.

His words are: 'Go my little children, live a life on the earth, explore your own identity, learn from each other and learn from yourself. You will come back to me with many questions and apologies of how you failed. No one is a failure. Some find it harder to learn by their own mistakes.

It is one of life's lessons, of which there are many. You are sent forth with love and you will be received back with love. The journey of life is a lesson in itself."

## Nature, Nurture and Religion – Aspects of Influence

Since the moment of birth, we are influenced by our inherent biological nature. Our resistance to disease, the health or otherwise of our organs and how robust or otherwise we are in our mental and physical health stems from our parental bloodlines. Enjoying full health or being destined to suffer with various ailments is one strand of existence that our spiritual journey has to come to terms with. Of course, parental bloodlines are not the only reason. People who have suffered in accidents or in theatres of War, have lost limbs have to find a way to overcome their tragedies. We see their human spirit shine through with courage. Their mental strength and determination enable them to cope.

A second strand of influence is how we were nurtured. This involves our livelihood, our living conditions and the way we were brought up. These factors include the love and care, or lack of it, during childhood and the economic background too. Whether we went to school, where in the world we lived, and the guidance we received all played a part in shaping the adults we became. In adulthood, job, family and finance can bring pleasure and pressure in equal measure. The fight for survival or the search for success focuses the mind on material matters. Also our state of mind, our confidence, our self-esteem, how we value ourselves, is fundamental to our happiness.

## Spirituality and Religion

Your spirit, your soul, your physical body, from birth to passing, form the essential, individual you. Never forget you are your own person. Religious instruction that shares the values of Spirit that cares for others, and shows genuine consideration, that gives love and positivity, will help you blossom. Religions that expect you to follow their rules and place restrictions on your heart and mind mean you not totally free to flourish. There is only one Creator, only one God. Whatever religious code people follow when this life ends, everyone returns to the world of Spirit.

Spirituality can enhance whatever belief system you follow. By receiving proof that consciousness continues after physical death, you will realise that life itself is continuous. It's as if you're adding rocket boosters to your spiritual awareness. It's like putting the word 'spiritual' to your self- description to become a spiritual Hindu, a spiritual Christian, a spiritual Muslim or to simply accept your fundamental spirituality if you don't follow any system at all. The message here is to be open-minded and respectful of others' spiritual choices. God gives everyone free will of choice that should not be turned against each other.

These words are from spirit:

"We respect every one of the religious beliefs that are formed within your earth. We would never disrespect any leader or follower. This would be wrong because eventually when their souls leave their earthly body they are welcomed with the pure love from our world and are greeted with the open arms of spiritual warmth. They all return to us in Spirit, to our world. When they pass they come to us."

Wang Chang wished to give his views on living this life. At one point he refers to the working relationship between Janet and myself:

"When a spirit decides to come back in the physical form it is not easy to plan a pathway. This is because there are two journeys in a single body, one physical one spiritual. A child is born and grows in limb and mind, while also growing in spiritual love. Your mind is the driving force of the physical being. At times there is confusion and growth between the two parts. Physical and spiritual can be at odds. There are times when they have to live within the life of what they are. Physical growth is where a person develops from child to adult with someone to nuture and guide you. When you are an adult, that all goes. Some find it difficult, the parent they used to rely on is no longer there. Some relish this change as they can become a free spirit. They can do everything they want without distraction. Within the free spirit there is a conflicting element of different personalities in your world.

Take the example of your immediate personal group. Within that pocket, there are times when you are on your own. You start to grow and learn lessons; for instance, how to defend yourself spiritually and physically. You give yourself protection. People build up gates or doors, or put up a brick wall around them. With these invisible barriers, you learn how to shield yourself. As you grow up you need to learn how to bend and adjust. Can you become free? At times, you are held down by others around you. Then you begin to sense an invisible pathway. Sometimes you need to let go of things and let them fall by the wayside. This can happen at any time. The two strands can grow at the same time or the spiritual may surface as you get older. The spiritual growth comes to the fore and develops; the learning, wisdom, knowledge remains suppressed until you are ready to come back to Spirit. All the negativity is sifted away and replaced with purity.

Everything that goes with the physical being is slowly being left behind. The purity of energy remains within the spiritual core. You may reach a certain point when you realise that you didn't gain all you expected from your personal relationships. They are falling away from you. That's when the door to your own spirituality opens up. You embark on a fresh direction and a new reality. All the spiritual knowledge from previous incarnations comes back to the front of your mind to be drawn upon. My friend, it is only a tiny amount that is in your current mind. It can't be every experience from past incarnations. That's why we sent Janet along as two minds can work as one and start to produce the work you can do together. You have your different attributes to combine. This sharing applies to many people on the earth. Some like to work on their own or get together with others to share. Wang Chang views all the meetings with great interest. Wang Chang is always there as he is part of the group. Wang Chang is a founder member of the group, first with Janet and then with you."

## Grief is the price you pay for love

We're nearing the end of this half of the book. We want to reach out to you or anyone who has suffered loss. Whether it is a friend or family member or a much loved family pet, grief with all its different intensities is the price you pay for love. The level and depth of our emotions are the measures of our humanity, of our love and caring.

A parent losing a child could live a life- sentence of mourning. The parent will never forget, but after a period of intense mourning they could lead a positive life in honour of that child. They could remember the love and joy and live their life as a tribute; and not a death-sentence of dread.

This message is from Red Arrow and has been repeated from our first book 'Being Spirit'. Spirit speaks from the heart:

"There comes a time in everyone's life when they have to experience the true emotions of grief. This is an emotion that affects everyone in different ways. It can be raw like an opened wound or it can be like a dull ache that is continuous. It can be like a pain in the heart causing stress and anguish. However it affects a person,everyone has one thing in common which is. 'How long will the pain last? Will it be forever?' There is no real answer to this because everyone has to deal with their own personal feelings in their own way.

Grief isn't only just about losing a person back to the Homeland; people can grieve for many different reasons. It's mainly for the loss of something that was held dear to that person. These emotions are part of the soul, for the person to experience life in all stages; whether it is the height of happiness or the depth of despair. How they are dealt with is significant to how you will cope in the long term.

For many, it's like a path that eventually widens out into a clearing, leading onto different pathways and allowing space within your inner being to walk forwards to a new start. For when you have experienced loss of any kind, it is one final chapter closing in your life; therefore, a new chapter is ready to be opened and started anew.

Difficult situations in a person's life can be a challenge and, to overcome these challenges, inner strength and courage are vital threads to be drawn upon. It is not always easy to stand up against an emotion that is strong, such as losing someone who has been an important figure in your life. The future in front of you can seem bleak but the dark clouds will eventually fade with time. There is no time limit on this; it is different for each individual. Memories play an important part in handling loss as they can bring back the happiness you once would have shared together. They can also cause sadness but, whatever feelings they invoke, it is the healing process you have to experience to move on and remember that person with the love that surrounds them. They only leave you in their physical form; they are always with you with their spiritual self.

Recovering from the loss other than that of losing a loved one also brings challenges, which need strength to recover from. The feelings and emotions are similar in many ways and are just as difficult to cope with. The difference being is that people around you react differently to your circumstances, sometimes making the adjustments to your surroundings much more difficult. When on the earth, you rely strongly on the support of others around you; it's important to have that human support there to help and give the strength,which is needed. People can be very fickle at times and can lose the ability to send their thoughts of help to those who need it; whether it's for the loss of a soul or the loss of something else but, whatever the loss, it is time that will eventually help you recover and move on towards a new beginning.

Life on your earth can at times be very difficult. Challenges are there for you to recover from and how this is handled is different from person to person; your emotions are you. They make you the person you are. Spirit can help but the strength is there within everyone. It's how you make use of it. It is your own personal pathway, one which has to be led by yourself. Mistakes are there to be made and mistakes are there to be learnt from. Your inner soul is your spiritual self and once a person recognises this then all can be conquered."

## Suicide: The two sides of suicide

It breaks my heart to write these next lines. I write of a childhood friend who took his own life. That was over twenty years ago and family and friends still feel the pain. He left a legacy he would not wish on anyone. Sadly, that's the unsuspecting gift of grief suicide leaves. After the shock you ask yourself the 'If only' questions - 'Could I have done more?' 'Why didn't he/she reach out?' You realise that in that terrible moment it was their choice, whether they were lucid, drunk or on drugs; they took that fateful step. To us they couldn't have been in their right mind. But we don't know the hopeless, searing depth of despair and torment they felt.

We do know that we are left to pick up the pain. We do know they are alive in Spirit and they feel our pain and misery too. We must still love them for who they were and the love they gave. It is love and understanding in this world and love in the next that will fuel forgiveness.

Let me explain that last sentence. Unlike the damning verdict of earthly religions, Spirit is not like that. There's no mortal sin, no burning in hell. When someone passes, they are still Spirit. Their passing in these horrible circumstances was a part of their journey. They may have ended the precious gift of life on earth early, but that was their decision and they will have to take responsibility. They will have to ask forgiveness and mean it. They will witness the emotional hurt they've caused. But, in keeping with the spiritual circle of life, this action was part of this incarnation and will be atoned for and learnt from. The trauma and heart-breaking lessons will be imbedded into their spiritual memory.

This is Running Water's view:

"Everyone has their own individual personality, sensitivities, goals, stamina and zest for life. Everyone has different thoughts, different values and different goals to focus on. Some can conquer all of life's hurdles. Some just cope and there are others who feel they are failures; a failure to themselves and to the loved ones around them.

There is no particular type of upbringing that is the cause for anyone to end their own life. It is the choice of the person. It can be a rash decision taken on impulse. It can be thoughts that have been harboured within that person for a long time, torturing their minds in a way where they can become bewildered as to what action to take. Some merely see it as a way out of a difficult situation. It is said that it is a sin to end your life before your time is complete. My friend, this is debatable as there are many different mental and physical circumstances to be considered. However, as it has been mentioned, life is a precious gift.

People cling onto life for fear of the unknown. They cling for the sake of their loved ones. Most people wish to live to an old age; they have garnered the thoughts within their minds that is it the natural order of life. When a person has taken it upon themselves to end their life by their own hand, many feel anger and shame when so many people are clinging on with hope and when their own lives are at risk through illness, starvation or the difficulties of just surviving."

Looks can be deceptive. Someone may seem to be okay but they have mental demons that are hidden from sight. We all have the light of spirit shining from us. If you suspect a friend is being withdrawn or acting out of character, put a loving arm around them. Shine your light into their darkness.

## Coronavirus Attack - A Message from Spirit

22$^{nd}$ March 2020. Today, across the world the coronavirus is on the attack taking lives especially from the elderly and those with pre-existing health conditions. It is affecting every aspect of normal life. Last night Janet received this message from Jimmy. We wanted you to read this as an example of how spirit is entwined with our lives. His words are exactly as received:

21st March 2020

"Hello Steve,

March on with your heads held high, that what I would say, at the moment, to everyone on your earth who has to adapt to the many changes that are taking place. Scary times, I know, but there is an ending to this and people will all come out of it in the end.

These things happen in people's lifetimes; occurrences come along and knock you sideways all unexpectedly. People talk about wars, famine, earthquakes and all other disasters that can take place but they all have one thing in common and that is they are all mainly secluded to one place or area, unless of course it is war that affects the whole world. But, then again, there are certain countries that are neutral so it doesn't affect them so, therefore, there would be pockets of the world untouched by destruction. This does not mean to say they would be completely oblivious to what's going on around them but they would be playing no part in the actions.

This is different because it's a virus that is unseen and has been able to run free without any attack from antibiotics or any antidotes to kill it, plus it doesn't need a passport to go from one border to the other. There are no restrictions as to where it goes, it has done exactly what it wants to do and that is to cause havoc all around your world. It has silently spread its destruction without causing any noise or movement.

It's not only making people sick in body; the effects it has on the world is causing anxiety, stress and grief. Yes grief; not because they have lost a person but because they are losing control of their lives, their jobs and maybe, in some instances, their homes and their reason.

We see how people are behaving; thankfully they are the minority. It is fear you see. Fear does strange things to certain folk; they act irrationally without any thought for others. They can only think of themselves and their own families; they cannot extend their thoughts out towards others to share or to help them so they let greed take over their senses and act selfishly.

Then there is the majority who are thinking about others, how can they help, what can they do to be useful to the rest of society? This is humanity at its best; the best comes out in people when times are hard. Just like in the two wars, many people surprised themselves at how they worked selflessly for others. They didn't want nor need any rewards; it gave them pleasure to be able to pull on their own inner resources to be of help to whoever needed it.

You are all being locked behind your doors. 'Why?' Do you ask. Is it so you can all isolate and the disease will diminish and you can all go back to what you were doing before, or is it so you can all have a good think about how you are all acting and what is being done to your planet. Now Steve, there's a thought, what do you think on that one?

There have been times over the millenniums and centuries when the unseen forces have had to intervene with the ways man has been acting. It's been like an unwritten script that there has been a bit of a hiccup in the smooth running of the world, so desperate measures have to be taken. You can see where I'm going with this Steve don't you? I'll try to keep to the point, what I'm trying to say is this...

However small it is, each and every one of you are kind of responsible for the falling apart and less interaction between others; what is happening to the planet, the animals and how they are being destroyed by rubbish littering the streets and countryside, sea life being destroyed by plastic and rubbish being thrown out to sea. Technology has advanced so much in the last decade; it's making development and progress much easier especially for many industries and careers. It's propelling many jobs and people into the future a lot quicker than they could ever have imagined, allowing people to fulfil their goals and go further with the knowledge it is giving them access to. Knowledge has become a lot easier to obtain, allowing many to advance further in their minds for many subjects that are of interest to them. It also gives people more freedom to be able to achieve their goals.

Then there is the other side to it. This is the bit where it's important for people to sit up and take a good look at what's happening all around them. First, we will start with the children. They are given a device that is much better than any toy or doll where you have to use your imagination. This device is magical, it can talk to you, they can play games, talk to their friends, they can write on it, send pictures on it, do all sorts of marvellous things without having to use any thought or imagination. It becomes like a drug to them where they don't want to be parted with it. Ever! Then they get told off for ignoring everyone else and not talking to people. Stop here and have a good think; who gave them the device in the first place? The adult, that's who! The very same person who is now complaining that the child has become addicted to the device and refuses to put it down. I bet you've never seen so many bald patches on people's head before, because they have always got their heads down either texting, talking or watching something. If you go to talk to them, you do so at your own risk because you are interrupting their concentration on an inanimate object. They have silent conversations where eye contact has been forgotten and any interaction with a physical being is ignored.

Your world is going at a very fast rate and the people within it are being whipped up along with the furore of it all.

It's time now for people to stop and think of how precious all your lives are, how nice it is to be able to sit with your families, loved one and friends to talk to each other, enjoy each other's company, play games, read books and talk about what you have read and learned. Go out for walks, interact with others, find a hobby and enjoy life. Yes, the technology will still be there, it has become an essential part of your lives, but don't allow it to take over. Use it for the good it creates then put it to the side and interact with the human elements you all have, rather than become a technology slave.

In desperate times, desperate measures have to be taken. You might be thinking 'surely this is a bit extreme?' but, trust me Steve, when things quieten down and people get back to their normal lives there will be many changes taking place within many homes. Out will go a lot of insensitivity and in will come more compassion for others; people will understand all the wrongs that have been made and will try to walk forward in life to repair the damage that has been done. It's like a big wake up call for your earth and all who live in it. Industries will make the necessary changes to minimise the destruction to the planet and the governments will try to pull together to save the environment for the whole of the planet. Many lessons will be learned.

Sorry for the rant Steve it's something I needed to get off my chest. Cheerio for now, Jimmy"

## Coming Next:

Can you accept an existence beyond imagining?

You were born. You live. You die. What more can there be? Could there be a world of vivid consciousness, a world of Spirit, a world of peace and love?

The living proof of the Realms of Spirit lies in the evidence of loved ones who have spoken to friends and relatives back on earth. This also includes evidence from reading the messages from the spiritual energies given in this book. We'll be describing what it's like to live in the spiritual realms without a physical body, a timeless world of mind and thought. We'll begin where the physical world ends and the spiritual begins, at the passing from one to the other. It is one life we lead. One eternal life we're living.

# PART TWO

# The After Life Chapters

# The After Life

## Chapter 3

# CHAPTER EIGHT

# Passing into Spirit

As the earth cycle closes another opens. We ascend into Spirit and continue to live in mind and thought.

Every returning spirit follows the same process after passing. The first is a period of rest and the joy of meeting friends and loved ones again. This is followed with the space for reflection, where every soul looks back over their time on earth to study their 'Book of Life'. Time is without measure in Spirit. Changes happen when a soul senses they are ready to be made. Every spirit has their own story and personal path toward the Divine.

There is no Day of Judgement. No sentence from on high. No purgatory or punishment inflicted.

There is atonement. There is an acceptance of responsibility. There is a need to forgive and ask forgiveness. Every soul has their private inquisition. This is where a spirit judges themselves and is not judged by others. This is a record from first to last, from birth to passing. It will decide their next steps in the spirit world. Moving through the Book of Life is a cleansing experience where the spirit is freed of the static and residue of an earthly environment.

I'm going to stop writing now. The Scribe wished to take over. He wanted to describe an imaginary passing as viewed through the eyes of a returning spirit:

"The Departure:

My body laid there with every fibre of my being crying out to be released. Thoughts in my head resembling some kind of prayer. Was I actually praying, did I pray before this pain racked my body? A voice. There is a voice I can hardly hear; it is soothing, comforting and strangely relaxing. First, the words make no sense then the whispering starts. It's like something that is only heard by you and only you. The voice gets louder but not loud that it is bothersome. Don't be afraid; come with us your time has come. A hand. I think it's a hand, it looks like a hand but then no, it's the shape of a hand being formed from the purest of light. It touches my mind then the unbelievable happens. My body is free from pain. I'm floating above my body and wish myself goodbye. My loved ones cry. My voice says, 'please don't cry I'm happy to go, it's my time.' But then of course, they do not hear my words because there are no words, only my thoughts.

I found myself as high as I could ever have imagined, feeling as light as the lightest feather, the colours resembling the colours of the rainbow but in the deepest and brightest hue. Is this real? I pinch myself. No pain, no touch, no body, no eyes to see, no voice to speak, no ears to hear, yet all those sensations I can still achieve. My mind is whirring, my thoughts go back to the body I had just left, I can't get in, it has done its journey, it is finished with. My mind is now free.

Then something magical happens. My thoughts are filled with love and are directed straight to the loved one who is standing there looking over my, now lifeless, body. My only thought is to fill that person with this new love that is surrounding me. It is like sending out a light mist to surround that bereaved person; it floats and surrounds their aura. They slightly shudder and then I know my work is done. I have sent my love in all its purity. My new journey will now begin.

The Return:

Here is my spirit, elevated into nothingness. Everything that is in the surrounding area is the finest, most delicate, mist. I can see, but can I see? There is nothing there only this purest mist. I can hear, but what do I hear? There is no noise but this very subtle hum. It's like nothing I have experienced when my soul and physical body were attached. This is pure peace, with the lightest of touch that you cannot feel; but it is there. The only way I can explain it is if you are floating amongst the finest and softest feathers.

There is the subtlest hum surrounding my thoughts. The noise I hear has no sound but words are spoken through thoughts. It is my family joining my energies to welcome me back to the Homeland. My thoughts are filled with love and gratitude for the welcome party for my return. They whisper and float around my energies with the purest of love. 'You are home, you are safe. We welcome you back.'

There is so much love surrounding my energies a desire comes upon me to distribute this love back to my loved ones who have been left behind. How do I do this? Think. What I should do? Then my mind remembers them feeling sad at my parting, that's when the words come back to me; the soundless words that could not be spoken, only the thought, 'Don't be sad, be happy for me'. I remember them. It was through my thought processes that sent the energy directly their way. Then a feeling like that of a warm glow floats away and is directed once again to the ones who have been left behind.

Now my thoughts are whirring; this is happening, this is achievable. I am actually able to make contact with those who are still on the earth. We may be divided by the veil between the two worlds but we can actually connect through our thought waves. My energies want to clap, skip, dance and laugh with happiness at the thought that, although we are separated by the physical, we are still connected by our minds.

The Homeland:

I've heard tales of the Homeland, tales of wonder, tales of peace and love, tales of the purity of the return, tales of everlasting existence, tales which were unbelievable, too many to absorb and believe. Did I believe? My mind is now racing away with thoughts tumbling over and over of how stories were building up in my mind of the departure and the return.

My thoughts are settling down now to the discovery that my energies are actually back within the Realms of Spirit, secure within the pure love you can only experience when back in our world. Clarity is beginning to dawn upon me. My mind becomes aware of what has just gone before me, of my departure from the earth to the return and arrival back in the Homeland. How quickly we forget about the security of the Homeland, once we have allowed our soul to be secured again within a physical body, to become a person who walks and dwells upon the earth, to try to make a difference to those who will walk alongside of us. That is over for my spirit now.

The eternal life of which you hear about is here within these realms, within our thoughts. My spirit will now start upon the long and joyous journey of evolving towards the purity of the light, towards reconciling with the Creator, the giver of all. It is spoken on your earth that, once you reach the realms Judgement Day will be there waiting. For a physical being to hear these words, the thoughts can conjure up fear and anxiety of what is to be before you. This awaits for me now. It is my time to go through the catalogue of my lifetime. To see my life flash before me with every flaw, disturbances thoughtless acts sadness, joy, achievements love, misery, happiness, humility towards others. It is a time of reckoning and of understanding how we coped with our emotions that made up who were. How we treated ourselves and more importantly how we treated others.

It is said that God forgives all. It is God that helps and guides you along the road to reconciliation of your own self; how to learn from your previous existence, how to forgive yourself, and to help you cleanse your soul for your journey towards the eternal light.

During all these happenings, my mind will now have to learn how to live without a body. To adjust to being just a spirit with thoughts that can be compared to living a life on the earth. The difference being is that our thoughts are not marred by the material or the physicality that is experienced on the earth. Our thoughts, in time, become purified and our one aim is to direct that love and purity back toward those who we have left behind, to confirm to them that we have only left them in body but are still very alive much within our thoughts.

On communication to our loved ones, we have a glimpse of the sadness they are feeling through the suffering of their loss for us. This increases our love and, by using the full power of thought, we can envelop them within the love and light of Spirit and hope that eventually this power of thought will be able to encase them within our warm glow and hopefully reduce their sadness."

The Scribe wanted to explain what prompted this heartfelt decision to write these lines.

"Stephen, through explaining the departure and the return it was discussed that it be written as if it was coming from the thoughts of a newly returned spirit. We want people to get a real glimpse into what happens when the soul leaves the body, how painless it is and how quickly the spirit feels the love and warmth that is waiting for them. We would like it to be placed within the pages just as it has been written from us."

*** 

The Scribe's description of the passing and return to the Homeland or, put in another way, of going home was something special. Other guides have spoken on the same topic. These next pages will help us better comprehend the three stages of the passing, resting and atonement period, with the input of other guides. As you appreciate, every guide has their own approach. The first is from a highly evolved female guide as she speaks about passing:

"No one knows how long a lifetime will last. People like to believe they will pass peacefully in old age. There are many reasons why a life ends early. We may be here for only a short time and we don't know how and when it will end. Many fear not being around, both for what they will be missing out on in the lives of loved ones, but also for the sadness their loved ones will feel without them being there. These emotions are natural. We all know physical life ends. Spirits that have returned know that spiritual life is endless. They also know that, on passing, you will always be a part of your loved one's lives by sending them love always.

Before passing, the physical body may be feeling pain, due to illness or accident. At the point of passing there is no more pain. It can be like falling asleep. The physical body gradually shuts down. Release from the physical body is euphoric. The soul rises from the body and returns to spirit."

In a moment , we'll talk about times when passing does not follow a normal, natural path; when it is untimely and often traumatic. In the meantime, Running Water will describe a spirit's return home, resting and adjusting to life without a body:

"It has been well versed from us that when the spirit leaves the body there would be other spirits there to welcome them. It could be family, friends, the Sisters of Mercy or a guide who had been with them throughout their life. Not one spirit returns to our world without a comforting light there to protect and welcome them.

It has been discussed that the main objective is to alleviate people's fears. And that they, or their family or friends, will always be met and comforted by spirit on return to the Homeland. When the newly returned Spirit has made the transition, their first thoughts are those of extreme peace and love. For some, it can be both bewildering and slightly confusing when they realise they have shed their physical body and are thinking only with their own thoughts. These thoughts are just as clear as they would be in the physical form. You have to take into account, my friend, that we are speaking of every physical being that has lived a life, the majority of whom would have had no recollection or interest in our world or what to expect when it is their time to return.

How does a spirit learn to exist without a body? We mention the extreme power of thought. It's learning how to adjust to this way of existing.

The spirit has arrived back in the safe hands of their loved ones or a qualified Helper, to give the love and peace required. After their time of resting (as mentioned there is no time scale on this time is for your world) they start their progress and journey. It starts with adjusting to the fact that they are no longer human.

Imagine you have no body; your eyes are closed and you are floating in the air. All around you is extreme peace and you feel no weight at all. Suddenly you want to walk, to place your feet upon the floor. There is no floor. You are in the air. You put your arms out to help you stand. There is nothing for you to hold onto. You are in nothingness.

This is an example, to help you understand you would automatically open your eyes and immediately come back to a physical perception. The spirit would not feel distressed or alarmed, only slightly bewildered as to how they can operate this new existence without a body. Through the power of thought they would still be able to walk, talk, run, jump, dance, sing, and continue to 'do' whatever they would have done on the earth.

You will hear many stories or information from a departed spirit, who would have been paralysed when on the earth, saying to their loved ones that 'my legs and arms are working perfectly well now. I can straighten my back. I could even do somersaults if so desired.' The blind person would say they can see perfectly clearly now. The deaf person would say they can now hear clearly. The mute person would be able to talk. The imperfections of the body have been left behind and they are now operating only with crystal clarity from the power of thought.

As we will continuously mention, there is no time scale as to how long it will take a spirit to adjust to the changes they find themselves in. It will just happen."

Running Water wanted to continue his points on adjusting to existing without a body and when their resting period is coming to a close:

"The spirit has returned. They have rested and now their mind has once again become active. 'I have no body. How is it possible that I can still function with a fully-attuned mind when my brain has been left behind in my decaying body?' Confusing? No, my friend, just adjustment to the fact that they, through their own thought processes, can continue to think in the same way as when they would have been on the earth. They realise that the body needs every organ to work together to keep the body afloat and that the time will eventually come when the body has to give up.

They then realise that their thoughts and mind is energy. And that, my friend, so is their spirit. The mind is the most powerful tool a person has. They would still 'feel' they have limbs but would know they haven't. They can still 'feel' the pain but would know it has vanished. You can liken it to a memory. They knew it was there and know it has now gone. They would feel light as a feather in mind but can remember how it would be to 'feel' heavy within a body."

The length of the resting period is influenced by the manner of passing. Running Water continues the theme:

"Every death of the physical body is different and personal to that particular spirit. You have to take into account how a person's life was ended; was it sudden, traumatic, peaceful, brutal, expected or would they have ended their life by their own hand? The way a spirit leaves your earth can dictate how long they will remain in a resting period. Some choose to stay rested only for a short period while others choose a longer period of time. There is no order of time; it is up to the spirit. There would be no particular, personal reason why a spirit would choose to lay dormant for many years. It is common at times for a person on earth to seek many Mediums for information on a particular friend or loved one and to come away disappointed because no contact has been made. Their disappointment would increase over time because they would feel that they had done something wrong. Why had the deceased not made contact just to let them know they are happy? That, my friend, is all most people left on your earth need to know; is the deceased happy? We have been instrumental in passing over messages from a long-departed spirit for the first time in many years; afterwards the sitter would be jubilant, that at last, they had had the confirmation they so desired.

How does Spirit know when a loved one is seeking information from them? As mentioned previously, many spirits choose to go into a resting period which can then prevent the communication taking place. It is possible for a Medium to say 'I have your loved one here' while they are in this state of rest. That would be the influence of the spirit sending out thoughts of love to those who they have left behind. Once the spirit has rested then they are there in their full energy. They are thinking of their loved ones or friends; they can 'see' their light, which would be the aura wrapped around the physical being."

## Children of the earth

Sister Theresa also known as Christina, whom you met in chapter 5, wanted to explain her role with the Sisters of Mercy. at the return to Spirit of children of the earth.

"I wanted to tell you more about my work with young children and their passing. Because they have been on earth for a short period of time they do not have to undertake the same process of cleansing as adults. Babies who have been on earth for a very short time, not enough time for them to be affected by the physicality of human life; their energies would remain pure of spirit. Toddlers and young children would have little to atone for. For children from the age of ten, they would be expected to know the difference between right and wrong and would undergo gentle cleansing. Sister Immaculata and Sister Mary look after the older children and teenagers, with a cleansing process that would be in keeping with their earthly experience and society they lived in. If they lived in a society that was away from the modern world, they would have one way of living within the family, and totally different from the temptations and stresses of Western societies.

We are always there to help child spirits on their journey back to our world. Also, with every passing, there would be three or four energies on hand to help those parents and close family still on earth who have suffered the loss of a child. A Sister of Mercy and an Angel would be there to help at busy times. Sometimes I would have had more rest when nursing in my convent on earth."

## Soul Rescue – Reuniting Parted Souls

On every other Wednesday evening, Janet is joined by Rosie who has found her niche in the practice of Soul Rescue. This is another area where Mediums here on earth assist Spirit. It is extremely important work. It concerns reuniting souls that have been wrenched apart. This is where so-called 'lost souls' are made whole again.

Passing into Spirit does not always go smoothly. The passing from life to the afterlife can sometimes be such a shock, so traumatic, that mind and body cannot understand what has happened. The mind cannot comprehend that the body is dead. Why? Because it has happened so instantaneously, so completely, so unexpectedly that the physical mind has had no time to die. We are talking about explosions, shootings, killings, accidents and disasters. The soul was brutally wrenched from the body. In that instant, the majority of the soul does pass into Spirit successfully. A fragment, a particle, of the spirit's soul is left behind. It was disconnected, splintered away from the whole soul in the sudden shock. The fragment stays in limbo between the veils of earth and Spirit. The fragment retains the characteristics and visual appearance of the original soul to be identified by a Medium. This is a description of the rescue process.

## The Rescue Begins

The session begins with an opening prayer, followed by Janet and Rosie connecting with their guides as they tune-in clairvoyantly. The prayer and preparation creates a calm and welcoming atmosphere. The spirits wishing to be reconnected would see our auras. Imagine a pitch dark night at sea. A homing beacon from the land flashes out across the ocean. Our spiritual lights are signals to Spirit.

Rosie would sense their presence and, one by one, she would see and describe them. We have no idea who is going to attend until they arrive and introduce themselves. They may be recently deceased or from way back in time;

young, old, male or female, they come. Sometimes they bring their spirit pets or animals with them. As we know, all living things are spiritual beings. Dog owners would not be surprised at that. Recently, a dog had stayed with its owner at her passing to crossover together.

The departed spirit would be clearly described as the moments pass. Rosie would speak to Janet to see whether she too, had identified the spirit. The aim is to encourage the spirit to follow the light that shines from Janet's aura. The light is the doorway to the spirit world. As they pass through the tunnel of light their soul would become as one. Janet often feels a jolt, as the lost spirit's energy flows through her aura, without effecting her physical body. After a minute or so to prepare themselves, the process starts again. The session lasts for about an hour. The departed come through as individuals or as groups, as you are about to read. The accounts give you an idea of the range of experiences and have been recorded in note form as they were on the night:

### Rescue Log Notes 1: From the Vietnam War

Friendly fire bombing raid on a Vietnamese village, killing both American troops and villagers. The troops stand to one side out of respect to allow the villagers to form a line and pass through before them. When they are ready the villagers approach, led by a mother and little boy and girl. It's difficult to say how many villagers. One man leads his cow on a piece of thin rope. The rope breaks as the man goes through. The cow follows separately. Once the villagers have passed through, the troops begin to sing to raise their energies. There's a line of twenty soldiers. Jimmy our guide, joins in the singing with the World War One song 'It's a long way to Tipperary' to help the soldiers pass into Spirit. Janet holds Steve's hand to draw upon his energy, that is needed because of the sheer number of people passing through. The troops speak as they pass 'Thank you Ma'am. It's a pleasure Ma'am'. The families of the troops are watching from the world of Spirit. They are joyful to be unified with their loved ones. Jimmy speaks through Janet: 'Our singing is to help our fellow soldiers and I've got to look after my girl' (Janet). Five more now. They all pass back safely into Spirit.

Rescue Log 2: 9/11 Soul Rescue

A group of people stagger and climb from the debris of the Twin Towers. Sounds in the background of screaming and shouting. A large man tall and big was the first to go through. Then a woman emerged from the rubble leading a group of seven more. Another couple and a big man; they are all choking from the dust. He started speaking through Janet: 'All help me God. Thank you my child, may the Lord God go with you.' At the end, a shaggy dog climbs out of the concrete rubble covered in dust and dirt. He is wagging his tail. He goes toward Janet and climbs up on her knee before going through. They thank Rosie as they go through.

Rescue Log 3: Young Boy, Window Accident

A little boy chasing his Teddy bear fell from of a top-floor window. The shock and surprise were so sudden he needed soul rescue. He was crying out for his mother. After he died, his mother was left on the earth for nine years. When she died, her spirit came to find the boy. Now they were together again. The mother spoke to Rosie 'At last, at last I've got my baby back!

Thank you.' His mother suffered depression and self-blame for leaving the window open. Rosie described the view from the window. A Mississippi paddle-streamer was coming down river. Below the window were troops from the American Civil War, blue uniforms from the North and Grey from the Confederate South. They were not fighting. The war had ended. The mother and baby son must have been waiting since 1865.

Rescue Log 3 Syrian War Bombing:

A black warrior, a red cloth wrapped round his body, tall and slim. Holding a baby in his arms. He is at the head of a line of men, women and children. They are in the Syrian desert by a refugee camp. They have all been killed in a bombing raid. A woman wearing a burqa is standing behind the warrior who has organised them in an orderly queue, all waiting their turn to come through to the light. The adults are holding the hands of the children. Someone is saying a prayer while they wait. Nurses from the camp are with them too. There are about fifteen of them The warrior leads them to the light and Janet jolts with each passing. The last is a young boy. They are all covered in dust, dirt and blood.

Rescue Log 4: A dog waits with her owner:

Rosie sees an old Collie dog. The dog won't come through without the owner. The owner comes forward and speaks through Janet: 'I had a heart attack.' Rosie is shown a woman lying dead in a field, with both dog and owner side by side. The dog came to attract Rosie's attention, to help them pass into Spirit. The dog was waiting so they could go through together.

This was Spirit's reaction to the value of Soul Rescue:

Wang Chang, Running Water and Adam, (Cindy's guide), all join to say how important this work is. There are just so many Mediums who can do this kind of work. Rosie has found her 'Golden Nugget,'in Soul Rescue, it is her particular talent and calling. The group working together has created the right atmosphere under the leadership of Janet to provide this service. Each of us is finding our purpose with Janet as our guide.

## Thanks from Lucinda

This message is from Lucinda who was a child we helped one evening in a Soul Rescue session. Spirits normally say their thanks as their fragment reconnects with their whole energy. This is a message we received approximately three months after the event. Running Water gave her permission to pass on her thanks:

These are her words:

"I have never done this before. My name is Lucinda. I find this all very strange. They said I can go through. You rescued me. Well, not you. You were part of the energy that helped me to come back.

It was the young lady who I felt very comfortable with. She helped me come back. They are telling me her name was Rosie. It was a while ago. You were there. I sat on your knee. I sang you a little song about a fish. 'One two three four five, once I caught a fish alive.' I wanted to come and say thank you. To all of you, because you do not realise the importance of the service you have done.

It helped me come through the light of this energy here (Janet). It is like the gateway to Heaven for us. Just imagine you

156

are walking down a pathway, a big pathway. You get to gates at the end of the path but they are locked and you can't get through. You can't go back. You see the other side but you can't get through to the other side, the rest of my soul is on the other side but you can't get there. The gate is made so you can look through it.

So you wait and wait until someone comes along with the key. Then all of a sudden the gate is open. It is a sudden revelation. You don't even have to walk forward. You don't see anything but suddenly the gate is open and you can walk through and you have a feeling of freedom. It's phenomenal, as you are back where you belong. The fragment of my energy that has been left in the void has been allowed to connect again. There is a sense of euphoria of being back together again.

I wanted to thank you for being part of that group. Because I met with the energies that are part of this group (Running Water's) I have been allowed to come back and express my gratitude. You will not be hearing from me again. This is energy I am not used to, so I found it very frustrating. Everything is heightened, the light is so bright and the sounds are like thunder in my ears. I wanted to come back and say thank you to you, Rosie and Janet. And I will shower you with the love and the light from where I am. I will say thank you very much and farewell."

Lucinda


## Coming Next:

Your spirit returns to a world of mind and thought. It takes time to rest and adjust to life without a physical body. There's a process of resting, recuperation and reassessment of your life on earth. There's no rush in the world of Spirit. You're safe. You've returned home.

# CHAPTER NINE

# Returning Home

## Spiritual R&R: Rest & Recuperation

After leaving the mortal world you are cocooned in a world of peace and love. It's time for some R&R and a well- deserved rest. You no longer have a physical body, with all the restrictions that brings. Your knowledge and experiences are forever logged in your memory. While you are away from your loved ones, you can still make contact to those you've left behind. You will continue to be a part of their lives. Your love can still reach them via a Medium on earth who can make the connection. It is down to you to decide when you want to make the link. Janet tells of people who make contact within 24 hours of passing to say they are safe and happy in Spirit with all their ailments washed away. Clearly adapting to being an energy force and spiritual being takes some getting used to; but that's what the resting and adjustment period is all about.

Flowing Rivers and the Scribe explain about this special level where spirits return from earth. We will say more about the 7 levels within the Realms of Spirit. It might help to visualise the Realms of Spirit as they relate to the earth. The earth has 5 atmospheric layers surrounding the planet. They are the Troposphere which is closest to the earth's surface. Following outwards into space we have the Stratosphere, Mesosphere, Thermosphere and, last, the Exosphere. In your mind's eye, imagine seven circles or spheres surrounding the earth. When you pass, you return to the first level closest to the earth.

Here's a short introduction from the guides:

"Level one is the level of return. You can liken it as the resting period for a newly returned soul. This is when there is much reflection on their past life. All the rights, the wrongs, the happy times, the sad times; what they learned in that lifetime that would be relevant or important to pass on to help someone in the future. They would be learning once again how to live life without a physical body and to learn how to send their love back to people on the earth. It's like a mirror image of your schools with higher classes, except there is a big difference in as much that, instead of learning how to read and write, you are learning to adjust your energies back to the spiritual realms.

During this process there will always be other, more experienced, energies to help guide the newly returned spirit. At this point, there will be no teaching or tuition undertaken; this time is solely for the newly returned energy to adjust to once again being back in Spirit and to reflect on their past existence.

There are many avenues or pathways in this level, with the appropriate help given by more experienced energies to help the newly returned energy to adjust. As an example, a person whose soul could have been taken quickly from their physical form. This can at times be traumatic; they would immediately be helped by the carers or, as people like to call them, the Sisters of Mercy. These are energies who would have dedicated much of their lives on earth to helping others and they would have chosen the same pathway once they were back in Spirit; that is, to continue as doctors, nurses or anyone who would have cared for others.

Those returning souls who would have caused distress and gone against the laws of your world would be helped and guided by spirits who would have acted in the same ways as the newly returned spirits. These energies would have gone through stringent measures of self-atonement and reflection until their energies were cleansed of any embellishments of negativity and destructive thoughts. As you know, all the emotions that lead people to act in the way they do on the earth are left behind, but their actions are embedded in their thoughts, which is spiritual energy.

This does not include those who have caused extreme atrocities by committing horrendous acts upon mankind. These spirits are safely guarded in a secure, dense energy which would make it an impossibility for their souls to be atoned and cleansed for maybe hundreds or thousands of earth years.

Love and peace are the key words for the spiritual realms. Our energies live within it at all times. It is the one measure that helps the newly returned spirit to adjust. The energy is absorbed in a protective layer of the finest mist, made of the love and peace."

Understandably there are many questions people ask about returning to Spirit. Here is one question that covers a number of similar answers:

Q: Do people carry their fears and anxieties when they pass over?,

A: Throughout a person's lifetime there will be many hurdles one has to face. Every life is different for every person who has lived on the earth. Everyone faces different traumas, stresses and anxieties. There are some who have to endure health problems causing them much pain and distress. Some have problems with their mental abilities. Others may find just living a stressful time. The answer to the question is 'No'. Like physical and mental illnesses, fears and anxieties are washed away at their passing. Blind can see, the lame can walk, fears are shed because the spirit has left the pressures,stresses and constraints of a mortal body behind. Maladies are a result of life on earth.

Newly returned spirits would be cared for by the Sisters of Mercy or helpers who have chosen to look after souls who have suffered in different ways. These spirits would be free from what ailed them on the earth. Their pain and torment would be within their memory; but would not cause distress in their spiritual state. Through the care and dedication of the carers they would learn how to leave fears behind as a learning experience during this incarnation.

When they are no longer living in the physical, all aches, pains, torment or anxieties are banished. How long this cleansing process takes is an impossible question to answer, for every spirit is individual. Some can take, in your earthly time, months or years. This care would be given through the healing powers of the carers. This type of healing is far more powerful in our world than it is on the earth.

During the resting and spiritual recuperation period one of the aspects of adjustment is how spirits communicate with one another. A spirit guide describes what happens:

"Once back in Spirit any communication from one energy to another is done strictly by thought alone. There is no need for any description to be given as to how their previous physical body would have looked. It's irrelevant to us. The descriptions are only necessary when evidence is being transmitted back to the earth, to give further proof to the sitter that their loved ones, friends or acquaintances are who the Medium says they are. Many people on the earth can resemble each other in looks; this is why it's just as important to describe the personalities and body mannerisms of a person. This information is more accurate.

Many Mediums feel it is important to 'see' how their guide would have looked when on the earth. It gives them more of a personal touch and can make the connection between the two energies stronger. With the power of thought, we can create this image to the seeing third eye. It's possible that we can create different images of how we once would have looked. How many times we can create this image would only be once or twice. The image we would create would be strong and can stay within the mind's eye forever."

## The Book of Life

When rested it's time to review your past life, a life in which you've made all the decisions determined by your own free will. This is an opportunity to reflect upon how you performed in your earthly challenge. What did you learn during that incarnation? What progress did you make? Was your spirit enriched? Now is the time to go back and turn the first page of your Book of Life, the record of your highs and lows.

"For the spirit while adjusting to life in the homeland without a body, but as mind and thought, they would be reviewing their physical lifetime through their Book of Life. If a spirit had done extreme harm when on the earth, either physically or mentally, they are withheld from moving on, until they have understood the implications of what their actions had on another person's life. They have to earn forgiveness. They have to forgive themselves for the harm they had caused to others. They have to seek forgiveness from those they caused harm to. This is why you may hear many Mediums say when relaying a message to a loved one, that the communicator is saying sorry and apologising for the harm and hurt they caused when on the earth. The apology has to be meant. They cannot be lame words; the words have to come with sincerity and truth.

This will happen to every spirit, in whatever way they acted while on the earth. Every one of us has, at one point in their lives, had something to apologise for. No one is exempt from upsetting others.

The Book of Life, you can liken it to going down Memory Lane. At times, you wish not to be there. You can't move on until you have explored every avenue of that particular time. Once lessons have been learned and atoned for then you can move onto the next stage. There is not one single step a person has taken that is left out. It can be interesting and, at the same time, upsetting for some spirits. To be able to view how they made use of the life that was given to them. How they wasted much of their time on earth worrying about the tomorrows that never came. How they wish they had taken more chances while they were on the earth, and how they wished they had taken other people's sensitivities into more consideration. Everyone on your earth at one point in their lifetime has caused some distress in one way or another to someone else, albeit whether it was done mistakenly or intentionally. It's an impossibility to please everyone whom you make contact with.

The point of all of this is to gradually cleanse and purify the mind for the development and journey of the spirit. This process has no time attached to how long it will take. Time is immeasurable. Every life that was lived was different, every mind was different; people think differently. They have different views and objectives and their spiritual growth and journey will take place when the time is right for that spirit."

## The Book of Life Affect

Understanding what is going to happen when you pass over can change your living life today.

We're only human. We make mistakes. We can also change the world. The Book of Life is not all about forgiving, forgiveness and atonement. The joy, success, caring and good that you've done are also featured in the plus column of your achievements. If you need to make it up with someone do it now, when you can speak to them and show them you mean it. This is the time to exercise the power you have to wipe the slate clean. Get any atonement in now. Wiping the slate clean is what the passing, resting and reflection process is all about.

Being forgiven or receiving forgiveness is often hard when close friends and relatives are involved. Holding a grudge against harm done to you, either with things said or pain inflicted, can last years. It festers inside. And it takes real strength to put matters right. It's worth it. You feel lighter and putting a stop to the acid eating at you is one less thing to stress you out.

Speaking personally, my father came through during a clairvoyance evening. I was sitting in a spiritual circle and three of my fellow members received messages from my father showing different points in his life. The first as a quite fit, younger man, the second older, carrying more weight, and the last was closer to the time of his passing with bad knees and high blood pressure. His clothing fitted the right time period. I knew him by his personality and his messages, each asking for my forgiveness. His parenting skills were not the best but he was impressive career-wise. At 18 years old he was a rear-gunner in a Lancaster Bomber in World War II, when life expectancy was only three weeks. He was a sitting target as the Lancaster top speed was 282 miles per hour. He ended his flying career as a Squadron Leader, flying Phantom Fighter-Bombers at Mach 2 - 1,473 mph. One of the images was of him proudly wearing his 'wings' badge in his Royal Air Force uniform. I forgave him a long time ago.

After resting and atonement comes renewal.

This is all about you, about self-cleansing. There is no dreadful Day of Judgement. No banishment. No punishment from a vengeful God. It is about self-assessment at another point on your pathway to spiritual fulfillment. It is about giving your soul an overhaul to see where it needs care and attention. Before this last incarnation, you knew where it needed work. The Book of Life showed you all the ticks and crosses. When the resting's over it's time to move forward again. You're not alone. Remember ,as as an immortal being you have the power of thought to instantly imagine surroundings and scenarios of friends and companionship. Any thought can be made real within the blink of an eye.

As you develop there are Guides, Helpers and Elders to help you on your way:

"There are Elders, we prefer to say experienced spirits, who will be governing the whole of each level, pathway, spheres or planes, or however you want to name them. They are not there to chastise any energy. This is where we differ greatly from your world; no chastisement is ever needed. They are merely there to help guide the energies along. There would not be one, but many energies helping in this way.

Who decides when a bad spirit has fully atoned? Again, it is not like in your world where a person would have to prove the undoing of their mistakes, where they have learned lessons of how their behaviour would have caused distress to others.

It is all down to the care, love and guidance from their Helpers, plus the self-cleansing process every spirit has to go through. There are no short cuts. It takes different lengths of time for each individual spirit. How can I explain it to you? It is that every spirit who transcends from one realm to the other has been cleansed from every human element that would have been in their thoughts and their energy is ready to evolve and learn. Then their new journey will begin."

The question is: 'What happens Now?'

## Coming Next:

Once a newly returned spirit has finished the cleansing process what happens then? Chapter 10 takes you through the soul pathway exercise, which is a way of saying 'where do souls go from here?'

You'll also read accounts of souls who had a glimpse of the spirit world before they arrived there. And we have an interview with a guide that may surprise you too.

## CHAPTER TEN

# Living in Spirit

Newly returned spirits may not be new at all. Every day, thousands of human spirits return home. All of them would go through the cleansing process to shed any earthly mark on their souls. Once the cleansing is complete, they enter a kind of spiritual sorting system. A young soul may be at the very start of their journey. Their trip could be their first incarnation. This may have been their first experience of being born of mankind. An old soul who has completed several rebirths over a magnitude of time, who is wise beyond our understanding, would be side by side with the young soul at level one too. Running Water has recapped a little on the lessons of the last chapter but then goes on to explain what happens next. Repetition is no bad thing:

"The first sphere is mainly dedicated to the earth's atmosphere. Level one is for newly returned spirit. Level One is likened to the sorting depot where spirits will be reunited first with their loved ones, then continuously perusing their life's story. They would continue to learn lessons that they did not learn on the earth. Some will go straight with the carers. When they have finished with that process then they will go through their

Book of Life. The most important element that people still on the earth need to know is that each spirit on returning will be met by family or friends or a carer. Every one of these spirits would have the love and warmth that is in our world and each newly returned spirit will be enveloped within that love.

Once that has been achieved then each individual spirit will have choices of what pathway they would like to follow. This is where we can liken it to your schools on the earth, where students progress right from the very early stages and continued on through all the grades.

You also have to take into account the spiritual understanding that a person would have had when on the earth. For instance, the majority of mediums would automatically know that the path they would like to continue on is the one where they can eventually become a guide or helper. In each sphere there are many pathways in each level. There is no actual time we can give you for any spirit; because the individuality of each spirit time varies.

There are many choices to be taken. It does not necessarily mean that a nurse will go straight into the Hall of Carers. They may feel they would like to try something else before they dedicate the rest of their time in that sphere. In each sphere there are the Halls of Learning. The strength of the knowledge to be learned would be according to the sphere or level you are on. A spirit does not necessarily have to go through each level in every sphere; much of it would depend upon any of the knowledge they would have had in past lives.

If we place the spiritual and the earthly educational system side by side the principles are similar. Spirits who share the same level of understanding are streamed into the same spheres, where they progress together in a sympathetic manner. This is a ridiculously simple description as they are a multitude of spirits, at different levels of understanding and attitudes, all developing differently over eons of time.

As Running Water says, there are many pathways open including not following a pathway at all. Not every spirit wants to repeatedly follow the incarnation route. They are satisfied with learning through the passage of time and float like a leaf upwards within the spirit world. And, as we know, there is no time in Spirit. These spirits have decided to literally 'go with the flow' and let the soothing peace and love of Spirit take them higher with minimum effort.

However, people who are carers on earth tend to follow this vocation in Spirit. Mediums, or people who are strongly spiritual, follow the pathway to ultimately become spirit guides. Others take a 'lucky dip' in returning to experience different lives and challenges, to identify the right pathway for them. The majority attend the Halls of Learning.

## The Halls of Learning

The description 'The Halls of Learning' immediately puts us in mind of ancient schools or universities with students rushing to and fro from tutorials. That image creates the picture nicely, except in a world without matter there are no buildings, only in the imagination. Nonetheless, there's learning on a massive scale. Singing Winds described the Halls as a 'thought bank' driven by intelligence of astronomical energy and size. All the learning there ever was or ever will be is stored in these vast halls of knowledge.

Spirit energies can visit these halls at any time during their evolution, to learn and prepare for another incarnation or to aid their rise within the realms. Spirit guides who are working with Mediums on earth can draw upon this wealth of knowledge to pass on. This may involve them visiting the Halls to find the particular cell of interest they want. It may be to help their Mediums gain confidence, or improve their vocabulary, or help them improve their understanding on any and every aspect of learning. Black Feathers spoke of the influence the Halls have:

"Imagine having a sudden thought planted into your mind; where did that knowledge come from? Perhaps a child prodigy has a special gift and continuously progresses to make great achievements. They can have a mathematical mind, or a musical gift, a physical presence developing into a great sports person, or a scientific brain resulting in advancement in the medical world. These are just examples. The knowledge has come from our world and learnt within the Halls. Along with that knowledge is the drive within that person to achieve success and to fulfil their potential.

It takes many earthly lifetimes for the spirits to learn and gain knowledge from the Halls and thought bank. This is achieved with love and patience. It is our desire to continuously teach and filter the knowledge into the minds on your earth. It is progression. It is called moving on and developing for the advancement of mankind."

Within the Halls is the Room of Scribes. This is Singing Winds' introduction:

"You have found yourself in the position of sharing many conversations with one of the Scribes. As for myself, my friend, I can only view through the letterbox to witness the vast number of Scribes working busily away, compiling the future for you all on the earth. The knowledge is endless; it is powered through the minds of eternal knowledge. It is like a vast mountain of words and letters all waiting to be placed in order, to be channeled into the various minds of wisdom."

Singing Wings continues to describe his visits to the halls.

"My days are still filled with visiting the Halls of Learning; there are many tasks still to be achieved. The Room of Words is still very much my main focus. The importance of visiting the room is there are still many words to be spoken and written for people to hear and read. Another room, which is to become a gradual visiting place, is the Room of Confidence. Yes, my friend, there are such places here. For everything that is to be achieved in your lifetime there will be a room allocated to the subject. My role of guide or spiritual helper is for the development and progression of my Mediums."

## Astral Travelling with Spirit

You've heard so much about the world of Spirit, but would it surprise you to learn that some people can get a glimpse of what it actually looks like? People who are highly attuned psychically can view images in their dreams, during their sleep state. They do not visit the Homeland – if they did they would not be able to come back to earth. It is like having an 'out of body' dream experience. The line between 'heaven' and earth cannot be crossed. It's as if they ae surfing between the veils. I'll let Singing Winds explain:

"My Spirit Brother, our handshake is in place.

I would like to talk to you about my days. In previous conversations it was mentioned to you of my time within the Halls of Learning and how it is being taken up with filtering words from the dictionary into the mind of Janet. This is proving to be successful although, as you are aware it is a slow process. This is how it is when working with the parallel world. We have no need to hurry. That is left up to you in your fast moving existence, where patience is much needed and very necessary.

This is done when she will be in a state of sleep; it is easier for us to be able to channel the knowledge and information into her mind when everyday activity is dormant. Although the mind can still be very active during the sleeping periods, we still find it easier to filter information through in this manner.

In this state of sleep, many people experience astral travelling. This is where the spirit can take temporary hold over a person's etheric body and take them on a journey through the astral plane. It is said that they would be taken into the Realms of Spirit. My friend, if we were to take them into the Homeland that would mean their spirit would be crossing the white light. Once that has taken place then, my friend, it would be impossible for them to return back to your earth.

The journey is taking place in the astral zone; you can liken it to a layer in between the two worlds. With a sense of humour we can call it 'No Man's Land' but with a difference. Within this world it would be peaceful and euphoric and, for the mind of the traveller, they would only be able to relate it to the spirit world because the experience would be like nothing you would encounter in your world.

Everyone's experiences would differ from one another. Here is a common example, as would be spoken from the tongue of a physical being.

"I saw the most beautiful colours. Colours like no other; there were the most amazing hues of blues, greens, mauve and reds. I thought I had actually gone to Heaven. The atmosphere was peace like I have never experienced. It was as if I was floating in nothingness; the lightness around was that of a feather, slowing and gradually falling back to earth except we carried on and on into the most beautiful sceneries. There were buildings, lakes, flowers, trees and vegetation, all of which was new to me. There would have been the sense around me of people, beings like no other. No fear, just euphoric peace."

Here is another example: "On my second or third outing. I can't quite remember how many, there were beings. In our world, we are called people. I suppose they are or were people. They looked just like us but with a difference as their energy was lightness itself and the feeling they gave you was one of extreme love. It was the most magical place I have ever experienced and any fears that are within me of leaving the earth forever have now vanished.

Everyone's story would be individual to them. These are examples of the astral plane. It is also on visits to the astral world where many people gain knowledge to further their development and progression towards the understanding of the Homeland. This is how people in your world envision Heaven or the spirit world, where objects and people are devised not from matter or the physical being but from blocks or forms of colour, so vivid that you feel you would get the sense of movement or touch. That, my friend, is an example of the extreme power of thought."

That's an account from a spirit guide. What follows is the experience of Rosie whom you met when we talked about soul rescue earlier. Up until now, she's kept these visions private, but feels it's time to share them with you from her dream state:

On the Halls of Learning:

"It was a massive hall with pillars of marble, beige tan and white colours. There was a dome ceiling but not like anything we have here. It was so high up I couldn't see where it ended, yet it was reachable; so odd. There were many spirit people but so much space in between which made it look like there were not that many. You felt like you're not inside a building, yet you were. Very strange, yet the peace and love were nothing I could ever explain in words. To say 'pure', does not touch it. If you consider your most peaceful moment, that moment would be chaos in their world. Peace is absolute."

On sleeping under the stars:

"I have 'slept' under the stars with wildlife. Lions, elephants, baboons, dogs, cats, deer, hyenas, because I asked to be given the opportunity to do this when I visited and Spirit allowed me to do it. The sky was a natural, midnight blue yet there was not the darkness of the skies we have on earth. The stars were so bright and reachable,it felt like you could reach out and touch them. And the spirit animals joined me and 'slept' with me under the stars..."

On nature:

There were trees and flowers that do not exist in this world and those that do. The images were 3D and of colours I have never seen before so I can't describe them. There were trees that were every shade of blue, lilac, pink, red, green, and brown. Beautiful lakes flowing with the most crystal clear waters. There were meadows and river banks

On Angels:

I saw Angels and higher Angels who communicated with me through their minds. They were so tall, they looked like giants. I fell to my knees and bowed down to them. My guide was present. I heard them say: 'What are you doing? We are all equal here, rise up.' I heard them speak in my head.

They did not walk but were gliding. I didn't see feet as they were clad in long gowns, with a thin, golden belt around their waists.

## Interview with a Guide

Cindy's main guide calls himself Adam. Recently, she was joined by another new guide who is in a developmental phase. Robert Langton was a leading surgeon and doctor during the Second World War. His speciality was as an obstetrician ans he was active in field hospitals in war zones during the 1940's looking, after pregnant women during childbirth but was overtaken by the demands of the battle field. He was a strong character with a powerful personality. Robert is in the early stages of working with an earthly Medium.

Cindy connected with his energy, to act as a channel to say his words out loud. This meant that, as the interviewer,

I could ask the 'Doctor' a question in this format and Cindy could repeat Robert's answers.

What you're about to read were his responses:

S: When you were on earth in your last incarnation, did you feel the presence of spirit when you were working?

D: I had to work through the war. People were praying and preaching. I had no time to think of this. I had lives to save.

S: Were their times when something happened? Something that gave you proof?

D: I had to think rationally. At the time, to my mind there were no miracles. I had lives to save. To my mind, it was all science.

S: Would you think differently now?

D: This is why I had to come back now in spirit form; as I have learned. With this Medium I could do so much more. I wanted to teach people. With so many people dying, how could I think there was something behind the veil? I had to come back to prove it, to realise it. This is my work now.

S: When you returned to Spirit were you aware of your other incarnations?

D: Not at first. I did not expect anything; just a blank wall. Dying for me was the end. So I had to learn and adjust. I was so confused. It took me some time to understand. It was like I was lying to myself. I had a long time of reflection, to realise I was wrong not to believe.

I thought my patients were talking nonsense to me about a world I could not see. They were dying. They could see the other side, I couldn't. I was so arrogant, after all I was a doctor.

I thought I knew everything; science says we know everything as doctors. When it was my turn I got scared, very scared.

S: How did you pass?

D: I was lucky, I did not die because of the war. I just died. I was too old, I just had to go, it was my time. My health was not good.

S: When you returned to Spirit did you meet any of the spirits you treated as a doctor?

D: I was grateful; it was their turn to tell me: 'See, we were right'. But it was not arrogance, it was only love they showed me. They showed me that they were right. I felt embarrassed, so embarrassed. But I was so pleased when I realised I could come back today. Somehow I had to pay back. I did not know that at the time. I was so arrogant as I was the doctor.

S: You had to be in control to show confidence

D: 'I love control.' I was powerful saving lives. And then I died and realised it was my arrogant self, my vanity, and then I realised that we are all the same.

S: Then you decided to train, to work to become a guide?

D: It was my way, my friend. You have a choice to come back and do it again or grow in a different way. I made my choice to stay where I was.

S: Will you come back again?

D: I have done enough, I've paid my dues.

S: And your soul is complete now?

D: No, I have not finished. I will be complete with this work and I know she will succeed. Yes, she will without doubt. The work you will do together this time around will be terrific. They are waiting (other energies wanting to speak at the meeting). I have to go.

The Doctor withdraws his energies.

## Overview of the Realms

The Group of Eight wanted us to avoid going into depth about the other six realms in this book, as they are a progression of learning and development. They wanted simplicity to be the keyword at this stage and to provide a basic understanding of the first level of the realms. This is what Shining Star said:

"Let's play a scenario where you are spirit back in our world waiting to once again slide down the chute of pure energy, back into the physical body. You have prepared for the journey of which you are about to take. You have noted all the evidence that you have carried back with you from previous incarnations; your energy is cleansed, your mind is ready. You have chosen the type of pathway you would like to walk upon, you are bidding your spiritual friends farewell. Now, here is the part that you need to understand. You are now on the verge of the two veils, teetering there ready for the leap back into mankind. You can liken it to a mystery tour, where you know you are going on a journey but, until you reach your destination, the location is unknown. You have not consciously chosen your parents, your location, or gender."

As time is not an issue in Spirit and is not comparable to earth. Our time can flash past in a 'blink of an eye' but would take many years on earth to pass. A returning spirit may stay, be cleansed and progress in Level One over many, many earth years. The other realms are platforms toward the Divine Light. They are slow steps in spiritual growth.

Eventually, as their souls will brighten and become enriched. They will ascend from realm to realm through spheres and planes of knowledge. At each point, their progression will be monitored by highly evolved guides until they reach the 'Seventh Heaven' and join the Supreme Being.

## Question Time

Our guides stand ready to answer any questions that occur to either Janet or myself as our work progresses. These are some that have entered our minds. The answers are from Running Water:

Q: When you pass into spirit do you automatically meet everyone you would have known on the earth, including those who you did not get on with? Can a grudge or bad feeling remain?

A: When a person's soul returns to Spirit there is always an energy there to meet them with love and reassurance that they are back safely within the warmth of the Homeland.

The majority of times, this would be family members or loved one. It all depends upon the relationships between people when still on the earth. It's the strength of the love that would have existed between people. They can also be met and greeted by many spirits.

There are people on the earth who live a solitary life style, whose friends or family would have been estranged from them or long gone. These souls would be met by an energy from the caring group. Once the spirit has settled back within the realms, they would then be aware of the existing love from lost family members or close friends and any animosity would be gone and forgiven.

This also applies to anyone whom the returning soul would have not gelled with when on the earth. Forgiveness readily comes when back in Spirit. It will all become part of the cleansing process when reviewing your life: to forgive others, whether they are still on the earth or back in Spirit.

Q: With everyone you would have known when on the earth, do you automatically know that you have passed back into spirit and can you contact each other?

A: Close acquaintances and loved ones would be aware of the return. The connection would be through the thought processes. It is not like when on the earth, where you would be having friendly exchange. It is the filter of love that connects energies together again.

Q: How can Spirit be applied to the world around us?

A: You often hear our planet called 'Mother Earth'. Indigenous people worshipped every element around them and accepted the pure wonder of Creation, the wonder of the universe, as proof of the existence of a divine spiritual force. Native American Indians, for example, sense that the earth has an energy pulse of its own. The earth and everything on it and in it are sacred. Every living thing - the birds of the air, the fish in the seas, and the animals on the land are spiritual beings. Mankind should live in harmony with nature and show respect for this beautiful planet.

You know the answer to this already, everything is done with thought, therefore the mind can create whatever they want.

Q: What does the World of Spirit look like? I mean, we were introduced to the Group of Eight Native American Indians in their tipi in the late 18th Century before the white man came. Does that mean the world of Spirit can appear as you want it to look?

A: When we have created the vision or idea of the tipi, it is to give you a full descriptive account of how we lived. Just as it would be for any reminiscent, for any energy, in whatever era of history they would have lived. Everything that is experienced when on the earth is etched into the memory. Therefore, when that particle of energy is back within the Realms it is eternal because it is still part of the soul. When an energy is making contact with someone on the earth, it is up to that spirit to give descriptive details of how they would have looked and also of their personality. To give a descriptive account of the area in which they would have lived is another form of proof of existence.

## Coming Next:

Remember these words at the beginning of the book?

Believing in Spirit is not faith. It is fact. Spiritualism is not about physical death but celebrating life. It is not about talking to dead people, because they do not die. They continue to live in spirit. It is not about telling your fortune as a fairground amusement. It is genuine help to guide your way. It is not about scary stories of the occult and negative energies. It is about love and learning, of peace of mind, and real contentment of your soul. It is not in conflict with conventional religions. Spirituality is a way of being. It is the way you were born to be.

You are spirit in human form. You are a spiritual being.

In this next chapter we'll reaffirm points of evidence as mentioned in the text above, to include the relationship between spirituality and religion.

## CHAPTER ELEVEN

# One Life Spirituality

We know it's asking a lot to expect anyone to question teachings that have been passed down over centuries even to go against conventional thought. We've spoken about the power of Spirit. We've explained the existence of the spirit world and described the part we play as spirits in human form. To many, this whole idea is dismissed immediately; except for two things: it's true and you can prove it.

We are all living a spiritual life. Life and the after-life are on the same cycle. It is the appreciation, the understanding, the realisation that the two are inextricably linked that opens the way forward for a confident, positive, self-determined future. Our spiritual development is a continuing work in progress. Knowing we are here to open our minds and expand our thinking will make us more aware of the beauty and the challenges around us.

Spiritualism has no male icon, no leader, no controlling body, no dogma, no holy books, and no rigid set of beliefs. Conventional religions have faith. Followers have guidance in their chosen form of worship. Spiritualism provides evidence of the world of Spirit, the existence of Angels and a belief in God the Creator. This evidence also includes the ability of Mediums to speak to spirit guides and highly developed energies. If you were to bring the core beliefs of spiritualism together they could look like this:

- A belief in God or a supreme intelligence and Creator of the universe.

- A belief in Angels, light beings and spiritual entities.

- The existence of an eternal, spiritual world of thought- energy.

- Human beings and all living things survive physical death to join the spiritual world.

- Spiritual existence is progressive, with the human soul developing in love and light.

- Every element of creation and the universe is spiritually linked.

- Mankind are caretakers of planet earth and should abide by nature's physical and spiritual laws.

- We must take responsibility for our actions and treat others as we would expect to be treated, in love and freedom.

- We are all spiritual beings. We are spirits in human form.

- Mankind should have freedom of religious thought and belief without imposing these beliefs upon others.

## Spirituality and Religion

On a fundamental level, there is no conflict between spirituality and religion. One major difference is that conventional religions are earth-centred, with codes of conduct and practices mainly developed by the male gender.

Spiritualism isn't. Spirituality is all encompassing, with both the spiritual world 'heaven' and the physical world 'earth' functioning in unison at the same time. Both are realities. One visible. One invisible.

Many religions accept the existence of an afterlife but it is not given prominence and not described as an eternal partner to our earthly existence. A spiritualist approach blends harmoniously with all strands of conventional religion including Christianity, Hinduism, Judaism, and Islam because purity of spirit runs through them all. In Christianity the Holy Trinity acknowledges the presence of the Holy Spirit, with the Father, the Son and the Holy Ghost or Holy Spirit.

Spirituality can blend with followers, becoming a Spiritual Christian or a Spiritual Hindu and so on. It is having a wider definition of their chosen faith. But with one that can be supported with real-time evidence that life is everlasting. This will be proved without any contention when they pass from this world into Level One of the spirit world. This is where their spirituality and the way they have lived their life is the central factor.

Importantly, whatever God or religion people follow they will find their own version of their faith in the spirit world. Followers should be confident that their faith and their spiritual figureheads of purity, love and peace are represented in Spirit. By the power of thought energy they will instantly connect with their faith.

These words are from Black Feathers on the subject of Spirit and Religion:

"Your world is filled with people, you are there in your millions and each and every person is different in colour, creed, personality. There are many languages, many different cultures, many different beliefs. You all make up the tapestry of life; a huge jigsaw puzzle, some pieces interlocking and other pieces refusing to connect. There is much disharmony from citizens who strive to cause problems throughout mankind, these are a few but their presence is enormous, causing many to suffer anxieties and stress. The wish of most is that one day the people of your world will unite together and live the rest of their lives in peace and harmony.

Is this an impossibility? My friend, I think we can all answer that question without having to put too much thought into it; sadly, the disruptive few will always pull the punches, leaving the masses with good hearts always wishing and hoping for the day when peace will reign.

There is one thing that ties many together whether they are disruptive or peace loving. That, my friend, is religion. There are many different religious groups throughout your world; they are meant to bring peace and love but instead they are the cause of many of earth's wars and atrocities. However, they give comfort to those who choose to follow their leader. It's universal that mankind need something to believe in and worship. It's important for many to be able to cling towards a religion which they feel will eventually reunite those who have fallen by the wayside, bringing that love and trust back into mankind.

Everybody is entitled to believe and worship the religion that gives them hope, faith and trust. It's a common factor, that when a person has strong beliefs in one religion, they dismiss others, for their religion is the only one that matters. Others have a broader perspective and can reach their mind out to understand the beliefs of others at the same time as embracing their own. They all have their Gods, their icons, that they believe in and have their own theories as to what happens when a person passes away. Each religion has to be respected, every person who practices and obeys the guidelines laid down by the head of their religion is to be respected; although, at times, some religious groups will hone in on people's weaknesses thus making that person feel guilty for thinking thoughts or stepping outside the line of obedience and also blocking any thoughts of other beliefs.

We now come to our world. We understand we are finally now classed as a religion. It is an irony that for centuries and centuries we have been dismissed where other religions have been embraced; our world and beliefs have never and will never cause wars and disharmony. We would never stop anyone from learning the scriptures from any religious beliefs, we would encourage them to do so. Every living being who has lived a life on earth, whether they have been head of their faith or a follower all end in our world; they are welcomed with an abundance of love and all are given the same choice which is to prove that life is eternal. This is proven by extending their energies onto those who they have left behind releasing love and peace, it comes as a surprise to many spirits when they realise that our world is very much in existence. They soon adjust to the surroundings for, my friend, they finally understand that everyone has been worshipping the same God, the Divine Light, the eternal being; the one thing everyone is striving for is here in our world. It has been since the beginning of time. It's the earthly being that does not understand this. You all spend a lifetime on your earth struggling to find that inner peace. If only all your thoughts could band together and understand one another then your world would become a happy place to live in.

Black Feathers went on to summarise:

Our world, our religion, we respect every one of the religious beliefs that are formed within your earth. We would never disrespect any leader or follower. This would be wrong because, eventually, when their souls leave their earthly body, this is where they are welcomed with the pure love from our world and are greeted with the open arms of spiritual warmth.

We would never force anyone to become a follower of our world against their will. It's true we can use our energies to guide. And we are there ready when a person is willing to join our team; but we would never force anyone or fill their minds with fear. We are not about gaining as many followers or believers as we can. All we want is that people understand our world, understand that life is continuous and never to be afraid of returning back to the Homeland.

This is another quest for you to put to the reader, which is to allow one's own mind to choose where they wish to follow. We only want people to understand our world and it to be their choice if they use the skills and gifts which have been given to them. If they feel uncomfortable or inhibited about any of our beliefs, we would never force them. We only want to be understood.

Peace and blessings upon you my friend, Black Feathers

## Seek Personal Proof

Spirit hope you'll seek your own proof by visiting a spiritual church to witness Mediums at work or experience a personal reading. If you arrange a 1-2-1 reading remember not to give any person details apart from saying 'hello' and your name. The Medium may ask if you have had a reading before, then it will take a moment for them to be in your company and connect with their guide or guides.

I was highly sceptical. I'd experienced a strict Catholic school where, when I asked any questions about the Bible or religion, I was told simply to believe and have faith. As an adult I expected more. I chose to attend a Spiritual Church in Kingston upon Thames in Surrey, England. They were offering a 15 minute session with a Medium, during their spring fair at a special rate. I had never been there before. I sat with a Medium introduced myself and waited.

She stilled herself. I had no idea what to expect. After 12 minutes nothing happened. All quiet. The Medium turned to the organiser to ask for more time. Not impressed. It was clear it was a waste of time. Until she made a soft throat-clearing sound, her eyes closed and she began to speak.

She took me through the last moments of my best friend's life in minute detail.

I was startled and shocked by the accuracy. I knew how he took his own life but the Medium mentioned details that were later proved to be correct. She had to stop as the experience was extremely upsetting for her. To end the session, my friend asked me to tell our friends not to be angry with him. I had no idea how this was happening. No clue.

That was twenty years ago. Twenty years of finding answers. Today, I'm working with Janet and Spirit and learning every day. That reading was my personal proof. About a month ago my friend who was always a joker at school spoke through Janet, referring to me said : "He would not be doing what he's doing - unless I did what I did." My friend was right.

## Eternal Life is a learning Circle

Earlier, we were talking about eternal life and incarnation. We appreciate that one of the issues with people accepting spiritualism is the immense, infinite scale of the concept. And the idea that life does not end but continues to develop in each of us until we are pure of spirit is difficult to get your head around. The thought is completely awesome. If our minds were pinball machines they would trip into override and flash the 'Tilt' warning. It's so much to take in. We need to get used to the enormity of it.

Yet…

If we accept that consciousness continues, the existence of a spiritual dimension, lets' call it a spiritual world, starts to make sense. And, if we are without shape or form, are invisible and exist in energy alone, then Spirit does not take any space but is part of space itself. We are inhabitants of a world of thought, of mind, of imagination. Hold this picture in your mind. Imagine our earth at the centre of seven concentric circles radiating outward. When we die a physical death, our spirit leaves the body and ascends into the atmosphere to reach the first circle. We all have differing soul ages on the spiritual scale.

All spirits are created equal and accepted as equals but some may have reached a higher level of spiritual seniority. No matter what level of seniority a spirit has reached, if they choose to once again follow the incarnation process and live another life on earth they would all enter the first level on their return.

The difference being that, once they have completed the cleansing and 'Book of Life' stage, they will proceed more promptly to a higher realm. Not all spirits decide to follow the re-birth route. They may feel that they can better fulfil their spirituality by staying in the Halls of Learning to improve themselves or use their experience to help other spirits prepare for another incarnation. And so the cycle continues to turn.

## Coming Next:

We've reached the last chapter. We're writing at a time when the world is in a state of social turmoil triggered by racial intolerance. The death rate of Covid-19 or Coronavirus is **b**eing felt in every continent. To top it all, we've reached the twelfth hour to save our beautiful planet from global warming.

It's not all terrible. There are signs of hope. These factors are prompting a long overdue awakening. People are thinking again about the way we live, the way we act and the damage we cause.

By living a spiritual life you can be that change. Together with Spirit, you can prompt that awakening.

That's why we've dedicated this last chapter to you, to your spirit.

# CHAPTER TWELVE

# Living a Spiritual Life

This is the final and shortest chapter. Spirit, Janet and I wanted to show our appreciation to you with this last message from Josiah. He speaks about living a spiritual life and being aware of the power you have to influence the world around you, simply by connecting with your spirituality.

Josiah returns to the theme of time passing and how, looking back, we can make the most of the present and future. We print these words exactly as received from spirit:

"Time runs away very quickly when upon the earth; it can become like a race, always chasing the clock. Each tick is a tick into the future and each tick that has gone before becomes a memory. There is always a fear in many people's minds that they will never be able to accomplish everything which is in their minds eye to achieve. It is the drive and compassion within each of us that, at certain times in our lives, can become a void, therefore preventing us from moving on. This causes anxiety and the feeling and need to rush can become increased.

Our lives are stories to be told in the future. Behind every person you see there is a story. Some stories are to be told, others just get buried in the past. What will be of interest to one, to another it will be of no importance. However we view our past lives, there is always room for improvement. Doors become closed and others open. There will always be tentative steps to walk through; never be afraid to experience something new.

You do not have to wait until you come back to the Homeland to have a review of your life. It's something that maybe people should automatically do every few years: to have a review of their achievements or non-achievements. See how they can improve upon their character towards others and also to themselves. It is not always others who have to make changes, it is ourselves. We 'the others' from another person's point of view. People need to look deep within to see their flaws and also to test those flaws. It's not a question of always passing the tests we face every day; it is the learning for the future that becomes important. The learning that is for ourselves and to pass onto others.

There is nothing more fulfilling in a person's life than when you can see the outcome in others of how your aptitude to help them discover, within themselves a gift, that may have been buried deep inside. Every living human has many gifts within. At times, some of the talents they have become obvious and it is easy for them to express that gift; for others, their talents are buried deep. It is a gift if a person can discover and nurture a gift within another, to allow that person to unleash their fears and share the talents they have with others. It is not always what we can do for ourselves, it is how we can help those who find it difficult to walk forward and make changes within their lives. It can become difficult for some to change direction, to learn things new, to open doors and walk through, not knowing what is on the other side: that is, the way forward. If things don't work out, then close that door and open another. Never be afraid. Remember the tick of the clock.

Your world is like a playground full of people waiting to be entertained and, for some, to be the entertainers. It can become all too easy to judge those who are brave enough to express themselves in a way where they are airing their gifts for the first time or just improving upon the gift they have. To sit and become judgmental is a talent that needs to be buried deep and dispelled. Everyone has different opinions: that is what makes up the variety of personalities upon your earth. It is how those opinions are aired, to become judgmental can become hurtful. To praise and encourage can give someone the courage to continue and move on, especially if they were on the verge of giving in.

Everything we do is operated within the process of thought, that important, invisible device which controls our lives. It is how it is used which moves us from day to day, continually making decisions in order to live. It's the mind. It is you, the person. Everyone has choices. It is how those choices are played out and how our lives are lived."

Your loving friend Josiah

**We close this book with our love and thanks.
Spirit. Janet. Steve.**

# APPENDIX ONE

# Meet the Guides

Our greatest thanks to the spirit guides within the group of eight, members of Running Water's circle and highly evolved guides who have visited us and contributed to the writing of this book. They were the same guides who helped in the production of our first book 'Being Spirit'.

The descriptions that follow show the character and 'humanity' of these guides to show they are not imaginary fantasy creatures but were once flesh and blood. As you read these pieces remember that in spirit 'thought' can assume material and physical properties as if they are happening in the real world. The guides have taken this opportunity to tell their stories, in spirit and on earth.

## The Group of Eight

In their own words, this is how of the Group would like to introduce themselves:

"To the reader: Our group has been formed in our world for many decades. We are made up of eight guides, all of whom have been working together for the sole reason to help guide and teach those people on your earth that choose to work alongside us in the capacity of a spiritual Medium. For the newly developing Mediums there are guides who are taught by us to lead them on their new journey. These would be trained guides who reside on a lower level, they are still being trained by us while they are training and working with the developing Medium.

On this journey we have communicated through thought. Our words are transmitted to the mind of this Medium who in turn will deliver it to the writer. These Mediums were chosen by us for this work for their combined energies and strength. It is a journey that will lead them further on their spiritual pathway.

We all have our different roles to play; we all have different personalities. Each one of us is here for a reason. There is the one with patience, one who is impulsive, one who likes to be the balance, one who likes to have hearty discussions, one who will push hard, one who has an open mind, and one who will disagree. Then there is the leader, the overseer of all, the wise one whom we all look up to, yet we are all equal. This group is a fine balance of energies that have chosen to work together in order for us to pass on our knowledge.

We work with many Mediums on your earth and we work differently with every Medium we choose according to their abilities. These two Mediums we have chosen for a project to explain about our world in simple terms, a project where it would get the interest of many who otherwise would dismiss us. It is a platform for people to work upon. If you wish to explore more of our world there would be more knowledge and literature available which would be able to widen your mind and interest, we wish you all well on your journey."

## Introducing individual members of the Eight:

"The Group have gathered once again and we feel it is about time we made our introductions. It's been spoken to you that the head of our group is someone famous in your world. We would like to take this opportunity to explain about this great leader. He resides and takes the head of many groups in our world. He is not the highest spirit in our existence he still has many levels to conquer. His Native Indian name is Tatanka Iyotake of the Hunkpapa Lakota. My friend you would be aware that highest status goes to the Divine Light, the infinite being. We do not have labels in our world as to who is better than anyone else. It's merely explaining the order of longevity back in our world.

He is a very wise master and has gathered much valuable knowledge which in turn he teaches to his pupils. These are other spirits evolving towards the eternal light and along the way wish to gain as much knowledge as possible in order to filter this back to your earth. It is the knowledge from our world that helps people in your world progress and for them to make changes for the future.

Imagine on your earth a professor of infinite knowledge. He takes great pleasure in sharing that knowledge with anyone who is eager to listen and learn. He will teach groups of great advancement, also groups going back down the scale to beginners. There is no-one who he will not help.

He has many helpers who work alongside him who also in turn head certain groups of their own. Each group undertake many different subjects, some of which differ greatly from one group to the next, but whatever the subject it is equally important as another.

To the right side of our leader sits Blue Flame, Five Arrows, Black Feathers, Red Arrow, Rain Cloud, Brown Bear and Morning

Mist who will be on the left-hand side, thus securing the circle. Running Water, White Cloud, Wang Chang and White Bear are guests of this group and are invited to sit in amongst us. Behind us will be our helpers which Singing Winds would be one of them and not forgetting Wang Chang's helpers, also there are others too numerous to mention but equally important"

This message is from Singing Winds who wishes to pass on this knowledge from the leader of the group. The tipi has been assembled with the members of the group. The head of the group wishes to extend his blessings to you and to tell you more of his life on earth:

"My dear friend when I was on the earth living my life I encountered many misfortunes. We were living a peaceful existence for a short time until the white man came and decided that everything they saw and touched belonged to them. They were blinded by anything that was new to them. They saw our people and our way of life an intrusion into their way of life. It was never in their intelligence to join us and be interested in our ways and learn from us. All they wanted was to take from us and for us to fall into to their way of living.

We were of the land they stole from us claiming they had the right to take away everything that we worshipped and valued. They said it was the 'new land' and they had a right to make claims upon it. It was our heritage, our forefathers worked hard to instil pride into each and every one of us. The white man called us savages because we were talking in our mother tongue. They forget my friend it was they who were the invaders. They ridiculed our rituals which we had been performing for hundreds of years claiming we were backward and was forced to learn the white man way.

We retaliated and fought against the injustice that was being put upon us. I stood tall and held my ground for the love of my people and the land that we grew to love. I was always true to my word. We were proud people. I fought and won battles and even joined their side to prove that we could all live and work besides each other in good faith. My reward came in the form of betrayal from the people I came to trust.

That was in my time. Since that time many moons ago people say they have learned from past mistakes and want to learn about our ways and rituals. Many of us have become famous names upon your earth. We are now looked up to instead of being looked down upon. We are worshipped and treasured. The lands we fought so hard to keep for our homes belong to no one. They belong to the earth. Our spirits and memories are embedded upon the soil that took so many lives protecting it.

My friend I came to spirit harbouring no ill will. I forgave those who betrayed me and my people. From then on every spirit that has joined me in my world has had to learn how to forgive themselves for the atrocities they would have committed on your earth. They have had to sift through every emotion they possess and learn from all the mistakes they made. Even I would have had to go through the same process.

To forgive those who have done ill towards you means you can walk forward instead of always looking back. Your spirit will grow in strength. You will gain knowledge and wisdom. You will be able to embrace any new knowledge that is to be put before you. You will shine.

My role is to teach in a way where vast knowledge is channelled into the minds of those who are ready to receive. Judgement is not for me or any spirit to place upon anyone. The day of judgement comes my friend when the physical existence finishes and the spiritual one begins. That is when mankind have to own up to the mistakes they committed when on the earth. The journey to the infinite light can prove to be an enlightening one where the spirit will truly gain a wealth of wisdom."

Singing Winds wanted to add his own account of the tipi the groups meeting place. He describes his entrance after being away from the group for a while. Spirit guides remember themselves as we remember them when they were on earth. This is true for our loved ones who have passed recently as well as those like Singing Winds who passed hundreds of years ago. During the writing of this book the group of eight held 'virtual' meetings in their tipi or in a formal setting of an auditorium. Spirit uses these mental links to help us visualise the proceedings in terms we could understand. As you know there are no solid structures in a world of mind and thought. It is the energy of imagination. Singing Winds is Steve's brother in spirit.

"The Tipi: It is quite large. The opening is to the right of you, in the middle it looks like logs but not a big blazing fire, on the floor all around the sides are skins all scattered around and in the middle looks like loose stones where the fire is placed in the centre.

Sitting to my left is Running Bear. He has a fur hat on his head (it hasn't got a tail) and a short fur coat, he is looking at me and smiling and says 'where have you been, we have been waiting for you for a long time?' I'm a tall Indian warrior, quite slim, rugged skin and of good years. I have scars on my face through battle. I sit down facing Running Bear and make a tribal sign. I would have been killed in battle and my name is Singing Winds. I was from the Cherokee tribe and of the character that nothing would stop me in my tracks. If a thought came into my head it would drive me along until my job was done. I was fearless but compassionate, impulsive and quick to judge, a trait that has had to be refined now I am no longer on the earth.

There is to be a meeting. I stay sitting and one at a time others are filing into the tipi and we do a strange hand shake. I can't understand the language at all but there is a lot of laughter around, the flap opens and in comes the leader. I know this because there is a lot of respect. He exudes charisma and importance. Running Bear is talking to me in tongues and we laugh then all goes serious. The leader has a long pipe (it's thin, more like a reed rather than a clay pipe we would envision). It is now being passed round. There is complete silence and peace. The meeting begins.

They are talking about past battles for land, they are speaking very quickly. They are pleased that I have joined them now after such a long time. The meeting is now over they all seemed pleased with the way it went. I rise and walk through the flap, outside waiting for me are others on horseback. They are younger than I am, my horse is ready, and I mount. After farewells, and we ride away."

This is how Janet described how the gathering assembles in the auditorium that looks like a semi-circular Greek theatre with aisles, banks and rows of seats:

"Imagine an auditorium above your head, it's like they put me in the ring and I watch all the guides file in. The higher guides take the front seats and the rest all sit behind. The head of the guides always sit on the front row in the middle and they fan out accordingly. White Cloud sits next to him as he is Steve's guide . Wang Chang will sit on the other side and I have Running Water with me in the circle. Running Water has to be with me because he is my guardian and protector. When a question is put to the group it's known that they argue amongst themselves and they can become very vocal. Other spirits arrive to listen and learn from the proceedings."

## Introducing White Cloud

This is White Cloud's first message that was channelled by Janet:

"My friend, I have been with you many years. I have witnessed sadness and distress within your life and the search for peace. It can be hard at times for us as a guide when we have to watch our chosen medium make mistakes, it has to be done, it is life, it is how people learn. We choose our time when we guide you onto a clearer pathway, it has to be done with your choosing, when you realise that the time is right for you to make amends. Your search has taken you along pathways of inquisitiveness and understanding.

I have been there all the time leading you from one path to another until we knew the time was right to bring you to your rightful pathway. Many times I remained a silent guide, the time is now right for me to introduce myself to you. My role within the group is one of a guest, my status in my world would be one of the same level as of the group, as Running Water is the main guide of Janet, I am the main guide for you. There are many others which include Singing winds, as time goes on we will introduce others who are an important part in your spiritual life.

When choosing who we are to follow we choose people of

similar character, we have many of the same traits, we choose like for like, this is so our energies can blend to the fine tuning we need for complete harmonisation. My time on earth would have been long in years, my status within my tribe would have been an important one where there were many decisions which would have been placed before me. We would have travelled at times for survival. That would have meant my one aim was to look after and care for others within our fold thus enabling me to hide my sensitive nature and adopt one of assertiveness and at times arrogance.

I wished and eventually found peace and contentment. We work together differently than that of Running Water and Janet, it is necessary for the blending of a continuous partnership. The Group are and always will play an important part in our journey. I will consult them many times where there will be new turnings in our direction. We are good leaders. We are there in complete friendship and will never lead you on a wrong pathway." White Cloud, Cherokee Indian

## Running Water

"I am known to Janet as Running Water, I am her main guide. We have been in partnership since she was bought back to this earth. My energies remained silent until the time was right for her to join us on our journey. A journey which has had its ups and downs, happy times and sad times, we are a partnership. Our energies have bonded and blended in a way where trust has been firmly placed between us. We lead, she follows. That is true friendship, believing and trusting. Her journey has only just begun, everything that went before was just a rehearsal until the joining of energies were entwined in order for the main work for spirit to begin. The work now has begun.

I am a Native American Indian who came from the Navaho tribe. We were peaceful people who only hunted for survival. We faced many trials throughout our lives. There was nothing we could not overcome. I had two wives, both of whom I outlived, four sons and three daughters and many grandchildren. My time in Spirit has been spent training and learning. Janet is my first Medium for whom I am the sole protector, her main guide, as I like to say, the one who pulls the strings. We are a joint partnership, we do not control.

It is my responsibility to protect her. She works with us for the purpose of channelling. We have spoken many words to many people and have produced much evidence. During this time, it was never my intentions to give clairvoyant messages. We in spirit only wanted to talk about our world and answer any questions. It was quickly established that certain people on your earth were more interested in their material life in order for me to develop with Janet that was the path that we had to follow. So my friend, for many years we have had many meetings in this way, eventually we put her onto a pathway where she could develop her gift in a way where I was not needed. This is where Tahonka came and joined our circle and it is he who is working with her with her clairvoyance."

### Wang Chang

He is on a higher level. Wang Chang is a guest of the circle who likes to teach. We are aware you have been acquainted with him, once met, never forgotten. He is from the Ming Dynasty and is a very clever and wise guide. You will have many conversations with him over the years. Wang Chang is his own master. He is an important visitor to my group he will come and go as he wishes and when he feels he is needed.

## Canuji

He is the most serious of the guides within the circle. He is very caring and a great healer, often the description of a Witch Doctor or Medicine Man is used to describe him. He has a team of workers who are healers and like to use old fashion methods of healing, grasses and herbs are his main instruments. His symbol is of a Black Panther. If you are in pain or ailing in health then you are at liberty to visualise this symbol, he has given you permission. He would have been placed on your earth in the region of East Africa. His journey back to spirit was in his second decade due to an infection from a wound in his arm. He rarely speaks now within the group but he is always in attendance.

He is very sensitive in nature and is only interested in the health of any person in the meeting or their animals. He is very sincere in the role he plays and will be a rarity if he ever imparted with a message. Occasionally he will impart information about the health of someone who isn't present in the meeting. His main interest is to keep people well in mind and body. He is regarded as a prince amongst his people. His costume of the skin of the Black Panther maintains his position amongst his tribe. He is very proud, they were proud people.

## Abdullah

He would like to introduce himself personally and has been given permission:

Welcome, my friend. It is with great pleasure that my introductions can be directed from me personally. It's never been in my favour to have someone else speak for me. I have always liked to be known as the wise one, the fixer, the one who can sort out problems for another.

When it was my life on the earth my geographical position was in North Africa, the country would be known to you as Egypt. My town has now been long gone, covered in dust and entwined within a city. My trade was that of a merchant in cloth and of many other items that would have been useful for the home. My other main purpose was that of money lender. People would come to me with all manner of problems; be it if their donkey's legs had buckled, or if the wife had committed adultery, or if they had no means to buy food for their children.

There was nothing I could not fix. People would travel for miles and days for my services to help them with their problems. Each night when it was quiet, I would walk into the desert and gaze towards the sky and consult the stars, the celestial beings. That was where my guidance would come from. The stars became my guardians, the whisperers, the helpers of all. I would relay any concerns to the stars and would be rewarded with the correct solution.

It was only when my spirit came back to this world that I realised that all along it was the help from Spirit. They served me very well my friend, so it was understood from the beginning that was my pathway, to help your troubled earth. My part within the circle is enjoyable, I like to utter words, and I like to give my opinion. We will meet my friend when the dust has settled and the time is right.

The specialist role Abdullah likes to play within the circle is that of an advisor. The main purpose of his intervention is to give everyone hope that although at the time of hardship there is nothing that cannot be resolved. Every argument or altercation has two sides and it is up to the parties involved to listen to each other with an opened mind. He has a huge sense of humour. The reason he talks of vast distances between his clients and himself is to place in everyone's mind that at times of distress and anger there should be a cooling down period. This gives the mind time to absorb all that has on gone and to be able to come to a mutual decision. It is a subtle approach in advising people to think rationally rather than irrationally.

### Charlie

Charlie known as Charles Short nicknamed Lofty, is from London's East End. He lived into his twenties and was taken from this earth in World War II during a bombing raid during the Hitler's Blitz. He likes to tell his own story which will be given to you when you meet him. He is the most popular of the guides. His great sense of humour relaxes of those who are sitting and maybe feeling nervous. His energies are those of a working class person who would have lived on the earth and through life did not achieve a high status of success.

He comes across as someone who is funny, cheerful and not too fond of authority. He likes to chat. He is and always will be the most popular of the guides who converse because of his ability to give everyone in the meeting a relaxed view of spirit. He is very clever his cheerful manner disguises how shrewd he is. He can quickly reduce any anxieties and does give meaningful messages although it can seem that he hasn't given a message at all.

### Josiah

On first impression Josiah is a solitary figure who likes nothing better than to sit in his room and write. Josiah has a very sensitive energy and always needs assurance that all will be well in the world when he is outside of his study. His eyesight is worsening after years of writing by candlelight with his quill on parchment. He loves nothing more than sitting on his veranda in the evening air with his wife Eliza or walking around the garden when he's feeling vexatious to calm him. He wonders at the beauty of nature and the visiting humming birds. He will be very amusing, wishing only to converse rather than give messages.

He can go very deep into the mind but at the same time hover above the surface. He only feels comfortable within his own type. He will automatically pick up on anyone in a meeting who is not genuinely interested in our world. Many people think they know all there is to know about the realms. Josiah will always be one step ahead and will not falter from letting them know. Josiah was a member of the Quakers or The Religious Society of Friends. He is a hopeless romantic. Here's a love poem written for his wife Eliza, transcribed by Janet from one of his messages to us:

"How my heart sings when I hear your voice
How my heart sings when I see your smile
You came into my life like an angel falling from heaven
You are my own precious gift.

How I smile when I see you happy
How I am sad when I see you sad
You are mine to love and protect
You are my own precious gift

The colours of the rainbow
Dance around you like sparkling gems
Through the clouds the rays of the sun shine like a torch from heaven upon your hair

The wind brings colour to your cheeks like apples
You are my own precious gift

You light up my life
You lift up my soul
You fill my heart with love
You were sent to me and I to you
We are our own precious gifts to each other"

*Josiah adds:*
Eliza would place all my words together tied up with
string and placed in a box and when she would be feeling
melancholy she would take them out and read them over
and over again.

# About the Authors

## Janet Neville

When twenty five years ago I walked through the doors of Barnes Healing Church there was not even a hint in mind my mind what was to follow. A few days before myself and a friend went to have a reading from a Medium, at that time I would call them fortune tellers this was because I had no idea or any interest in thoughts of the afterlife. In the reading she told me that my pathway in life would become very spiritual and that I would walk along a very deep and meaningful journey with many guides. Once outside her house laughter took the better of us because that was not what we were expecting to hear.

I wasn't bargaining on the force of the unseen forces that were to become my lifelong friends, so on the Sunday out of curiosity there we both were sitting in the pews of this lovely church wondering what on earth I was doing there. If I were to continue from everything that has happened to me since the words would run into another volume.

The journey has become a most wonderful experience that has given me a lot of joy, pleasure and hope working alongside these invisible friends of mine. My main guide is Running Water, his tolerance and patience has paid up dividends, he is of the gentlest energy who has guided me through years of teaching, learning and understanding.

The first few years were taken up with channelling; this is where Running Water's energy uses my voice to allow verbal conversations to take place. These are messages from deceased spirits sent to loved ones left on earth. They are also messages of hope and enlightenment about the world of spirit. During this time other energies who channelled through me have become my lifelong friends.

When they felt it was time I was directed to a circle in Kingston spiritual church to develop as a spiritual medium to work clairvoyantly and to develop as a platform medium. After about four years I left the circle and eventually started to work on the platform in many of the churches and centres.

In 2016 my life was to change once again. My friend Bernadete asked if I would give a demonstration of mediumship for her two circles, it was Christmas time and she thought it would be nice to have a service just for them, she also invited along Steve, who at that time was a complete stranger to me. After the meeting he approached me with an idea of the two of us joining forces to produce a book about how we are all spirits in a physical body and explain about the spiritual realms. So another journey began. Since then our lives have become a triangle of work, that is myself, Steve and spirit, we have written our first book Being Spirit the second one is nearly finished. Together we have groups where we help others to develop and progress on their paths for spirit. The whole experience is one of enjoyment, dedication and fulfilment and one of which will continue right up until it is my time go back to the spirit.

## Steve Bridger

In Janet, Spirit has someone with years of high level experience as a Spiritual Medium. She is the communication channel between our two worlds. My role was to pass on those messages using the spoken and written word. The two of us working together would draw on our skills from separate lives to follow the spiritual plan and walk the spiritual path.

Janet is the lynch pin receiving and writing all the message content. I help designing the narrative flow and work out the chapter order and content. My mediumship is the way spirit help my fingers as they hit the computer keyboard and put ideas into my mind for the books, blogs, website, when we appear in public and with the words that spirit put into my mouth.

Without going into too much detail, I started my communication career working in advertising with Young & Rubicam an American agency , then with Collett Dickenson Pearce – CDP with offices in London. In the years that followed I worked with other marketing agencies along with writing short stories for the fun of it. I've written four books with Believe in Spirit being the fifth. My first book was business related for people wanting to start their own business it was titled 'Success before Start Up' the second was an action thriller based in Singapore called 'One Degree North'. The third was 'Transform your Communication Skills' a book that helped people learn to overcome nerves and speak in public and improve their overall skills. The fourth 'Being Spirit' is a general introduction to spirituality. 'Believe in Spirit' is where you come in.

For a time I worked as a roadie for rock bands touring Europe, the Middle East and Africa. I was also part of a yacht delivery crew sailing a ninety foot yacht across the Atlantic Ocean from Gibraltar to Antigua. I went to RAF Changi Grammar School in Singapore.

Please Contact Us:

Email: spirit@beingspirits.com
Website: https://www.beingspirits.com
Facebook: https://www.facebook.com/beingspiritbook/

Lightning Source UK Ltd.
Milton Keynes UK
UKHW011828270721
387841UK00001B/224